THE 1982-1984 EXCAVATIONS AT LAS COLINAS

RESEARCH DESIGN

David A. Gregory
Fred L. Nials
Patricia L. Crown
Lynn S. Teague
David A. Phillips, Jr.

Edited by
Carol Ann Heathington
and
David A. Gregory

Prepared for
The Arizona Department of Transportation
Contract 82-10
Project I-10-2(86)

Cultural Resource Management Division
Arizona State Museum
University of Arizona

1985

Archaeological Series 162, Volume 1

Funding for the publication of this volume was provided by the Arizona Department of Transportation in cooperation with the Federal Highways Administration.

CONTENTS

FIGURES

TABLES

PREFACE

This volume presents the research design constructed to guide both the field work and analysis stages of the Las Colinas Project. It is the first in a series of seven volumes covering the project; the remaining volumes will document and interpret the substantive results of the research. The seven volumes are collectively designated as *Arizona State Museum Archaeological Series* 162.

The Las Colinas Project was conducted by the Cultural Resource Management Division of the Arizona State Museum, under my direction. The work was performed under the provisions of Contract 82-10, Project I-10-2(86) with the Arizona Department of Transportation, and was sponsored by that agency, in cooperation with the Federal Highways Administration. In accordance with state and federal laws, the project was designed to mitigate the impacts to archaeological resources which would result from the construction of a segment of Interstate Highway 10. The primary focus of the project was on the large Sedentary and Clasic period Hohokam site of Las Colinas, AZ T:12:10 (ASM), but work was also undertaken at AZ T:12:38 (ASM), a much smaller site located within the freeway corridor and some 3 kilometers west of Las Colinas. Excavations at Las Colinas were accomplished during two field seasons, from September 1982 to April 1983, and from October 1983 to February 1984; the second field season was necessitated by the addition of some 10,000 square meters of new right-of-way to the project area, an alteration in the scope of work which occurred in April of 1983, as the originally proposed field work was nearing completion. Field studies of the canals and related features at the site were conducted during June and July of 1983 under the direction of Fred L. Nials. A field laboratory operated during both field seasons, and in-house analyses of the materials recovered began in February of 1983 and were completed in August of 1984.

The original research design was submitted to the Arizona Department of Transportation in June of 1982 as a part of the technical proposal for work at Las Colinas and at AZ T:12:38 (ASM). An addendum to the original document was requested by the Arizona Department of Transportation at the behest of the project's peer review panel (Steven LeBlanc, John Clonts, William Doelle, George Gumerman, Albert Schroeder, and Ward Weakly), to expand and clarify the specific methods and procedures to be used in addressing the questions posed in the research design. The brief addendum was prepared during the first weeks of field work and its contents have been edited into the appropriate sections of the original document without specific notation; neither the major problem domains nor the specific research questions was altered by the addendum, nor were any changes made in the research design as a result of the added right-of-way mentioned above.

A number of editorial changes have been made in the original document. In order to make the format of this document consistent with others in the report series, the five major sections have been made into numbered chapters. Some headings have been deleted and others added, and errors in grammar, syntax, and spelling have been corrected. The figures included here are essentially the same as those in the original research design; several have been combined and redrafted for the sake of parsimony and others have been modified in the interest of clarity. For example, Figure 1.1 originally showed only the location of platform mound sites, without labelling them; the numbers and the corresponding list of site names have been added. Several manuscripts that were incomplete or unpublished at the time the research design was written have since been completed or published; references to those works have been updated to reflect their current status. Every effort has been made to insure that editorial changes have not in any way altered the content or intent of the original document.

The research design presented here was the basic working document used during both the fieldwork and analysis stages of the project. All staff members had copies of the research design, were thoroughly familiar with it, and were expected to structure field decisions and analyses in a manner consistent with both the general orientation and particular methods and techniques outlined in the research design. Field decisions concerning situations not specifically covered by the research design were made after consultation and discussion between the project director and the staff. Such decisions often brought into play information contained in three other documents: the research design written to guide the earlier testing of the site (Gregory and McGuire 1982), the report on the findings of that testing program (Schreiber and others

1981), and the report on the excavations conducted at Mound 8 in 1968 by the Arizona State Museum (Hammack and Sullivan 1981). The reader's understanding of this research design and of the subsequent volumes in the report series will be enhanced by a familiarity with these reports.

The research proposed and carried out in conjunction with the Las Colinas Project reflects a number of general concerns now current in Hohokam studies. The opportunity to investigate Las Colinas was a particularly welcome one in this regard, in that it constituted an ideal context in which to address a wide range of problems having general significance. Because of the identity of the site as a large platform mound village occupied throughout the Sedentary and Classic periods and located on one of the major canal systems, it was predictable that the excavations there would provide significant new information concerning the nature of Hohokam society during these two periods and during the important transition between them. The general problem domains formulated to guide the research reflect these expectations, and it may be noted that the site met or exceeded them in most respects.

The influence of the research design on the substantive results of the Las Colinas investigations may be perceived throughout the materials presented in the report series; the reader who proceeds from the research design through the presentation of the substantive results will recognize a close correspondence between the original conception of the proposed research and that which was ultimately carried out. Digressions from the directions and procedures outlined in the research design are noted and discussed in the appropriate chapters in these volumes; in particular, Chapter 2 of Volume 2 deals at some length with important changes in the excavation strategies used. Systematic consideration of the results of project research in terms of the general problem domains and specific research questions delineated in the research design is provided in Volume 6 of the report series. The appropriateness and efficacy of the approaches taken may be assessed in terms of these results and, ultimately, in terms of the degree to which the findings of the research withstand the test of time. Admitting some unavoidable bias, I would make no greater claim than to state that the research design presented here served its purpose well and was a useful tool for those who were guided by it.

Many individuals contributed in a variety of ways to the development of this research design. My colleagues in the Cultural Resource Management Division of the Arizona State Museum—Susan Brew, Jon Czaplicki, Bruce Huckell, and Lynn Teague—all served at one time or another as sounding boards for ideas and perspectives that ultimately found their way into this document. Patricia Crown, Teague, and David Wilcox provided invaluable moral and practical support during the hectic and sometimes difficult period that always seems to precede the submission of a major proposal, and the work could certainly not have been completed on time without them. Crown and Wilcox in particular participated in numerous late-night discussions of many of the ideas which were eventually incorporated in the research design. The substantive contributions of Crown and Teague are also recognized by their roles as coauthors of the volume. Fred Nials authored the portion of the research design dealing with the study of the canals and canal systems and ultimately carried out this aspect of the project research. Discussions with Suzannne K. Fish, Donald A. Graybill, Charles Miksicek, and Christine Szuter aided in the development of the portions of the research design dealing with environmental and subsistence studies. As Assistant Project Director, David A. Phillips, Jr. was responsible for the development of the addendum to the research design produced during the first field season. Benjamin Smith accomplished the initial editing of the volume, while Carol Heathington performed the lion's share of the subsequent editorial duties, with some minor assistance from me. Heathington was also responsible for much of the word processing and all of the mechanical transfer of information to the typesetter. Her always conscientious attention to detail is gratefully acknowledged. The publication of this volume has been funded by the Arizona Department of Transportation in cooperation with the Federal Highways Administration, and their support is greatly appreciated.

David A. Gregory
Project Director
September 1985
Tucson, Arizona

Chapter 1

BACKGROUND AND PREVIOUS RESEARCH

The research design for the proposed data recovery at Las Colinas, AZ:T:12:10 (ASM), is organized and presented in five chapters. The first chapter reviews information dealing with the former nature and extent of the site, the relationship of the site to phenomena represented by and within other Hohokam sites, and the nature of the sample represented by the freeway corridor. This discussion lays the groundwork for an understanding of the orientation and significance of the proposed research. The major problem domains and research questions that will guide research at the site are considered in Chapters 2 and 3; Chapter 4 outlines those topics with respect to AZ T:12:38 (ASM). The basic data recovery strategies to be employed in the collection and analysis of data relevant to those research problems are outlined in Chapter 5.

In order to place the proposed research in proper perspective and to create the broader context in which the research will be relevant, it is necessary to review the general characteristics of the site of Las Colinas. This will include a brief consideration of the size of the site, the periods and duration of its occupation, the character and distribution of features and deposits within the site, and its relationship to other sites which exhibit similar characteristics. It is also necessary to consider the nature of the sample represented by the freeway corridor, including the relationship of the corridor to the former extent of the site and the features and deposits known or predicted to exist within the corridor.

It should be noted that quite similar concerns were posed and addressed in the research design constructed to guide the testing program conducted at Las Colinas (Gregory and McGuire 1982). Detailed discussions of the former extent of the site, the relationship of the I-10 corridor to the site, and the postoccupational processes which have affected the site may be found in that document. Many of the points covered in the research design for the testing program must be repeated or referred to here, though they are augmented by new data recovered during that testing and by other comparative data.

The Former Nature and Extent of Las Colinas

Alphonse Pinart, the French geographer, was perhaps the first professional scientist to record his observations of the site of Las Colinas, and the only one to see the site prior to agricultural use of the area. During his 1876 journeys in Arizona, he visited the site, briefly described the mounds and the ballcourt, and noted that the site was "much more extensive" than Pueblo Grande, which he had previously visited (Pinart 1962: 35). Following Pinart, a number of professional archaeologists and other interested observers either visited or worked briefly at the site in the years during which most of the major features were lost to the processes of urban growth and agricultural land use (Patrick 1903; Moorehead 1906; Fewkes 1909; Turney 1929; Midvale n.d.). With the exception of Mound 8 and a small remnant of Mound 7, the major architectural features at the site had been largely destroyed by 1930 (Gregory and McGuire 1982). Thus, the observations of these early individuals are the only source of information concerning the former character and extent of the site.

The information provided by these workers has been compiled and analyzed elsewhere (Gregory and McGuire 1982: 25-46). It shows that Las Colinas was a very large, primarily Classic period site, covering between 1.3 and 1.9 square miles. Twelve mounds were once present at the site, and a careful evaluation of the available data shows that at least four of these were platform mounds. The others probably represented the remains of trash mounds or compounds without platform mounds, although the data regarding most of them are lamentably incomplete.

All of the major features at Las Colinas, and most of the minor ones, lay to the north of the lengthy Canal Number 5, or Canal Colinas (Turney 1929), and were situated some three miles west of the head of that canal, 3 to 5 miles north of the Salt River. The site was located immediately west of the terminuses of three branches of the Second Canal System, while another branch of that system terminated due north of the site. The large, northernmost canal of the Second Canal System passed "above" the site some 2 miles to the north. Thus the major canals in the area formed an arc or "U" opening to the west around the site (Gregory and McGuire 1982, Fig. 3.5; Turney 1929).

Comparison with Other Classic Period Platform Mound Sites

Further light may be shed on the character of Las Colinas by comparing it with other Classic period Hohokam sites with platform mounds. Although many of these sites and their impressive mounds are now destroyed—lost to the processes of urban growth and agricultural development—the combined efforts of early observers of the archaeology of the region and modern archaeologists have produced a substantial, if uneven, body of data concerning this class of site. Recent compilation and analysis of these data have produced a better understanding of the absolute number of such sites that once existed and their distribution, and have revealed several interesting aspects of their internal patterning (Gregory 1982).

The existing body of data shows that there were at least 38 Classic period sites in the Phoenix Basin at which platform mounds were built. Accounting for those sites having more than one mound, a total of 42 individual mounds is known to have existed. Some form of metric data exists for 30 of these 42 mounds. For each of the remaining 12, there is sufficient evidence in the form of photographs or descriptions, or both, to demonstrate that a platform mound did exist, but little more. The distribution of Classic period sites with platform mounds in the Phoenix Basin is shown in Figure 1.1. Data from these 38 sites form the basis for the following comparison.

Classic Period Platform Mound Morphology

As other workers have pointed out, a consistent form of platform mound construction appears to characterize the majority of mounds built during the Classic period in the Phoenix Basin (Schroeder 1953: 175-177; Hayden 1957; Doyel 1974): a rectangular retaining wall of coursed caliche was built, filled with trash, sterile soil, or some combination of these and possibly other materials, and then capped. This type of mound construction is found at Mound 8 at Las Colinas, and Moorehead's description of Mound 4 suggested that it, too, was constructed in this manner (Moorehead 1906). In some cases internal walls were added, creating roomlike cells within the outer retaining wall. Such internal cells occurred in the mounds at La Ciudad, Pueblo Grande, and probably many other mounds, possibly including those at Casa Blanca and Adamsville (Fewkes 1907: 319, 922). Doyel has suggested the likely hypothesis that these internal cells served to equalize the massive weight of the fill against the outer retaining wall. In some cases, the internal cells were apparently unnecessary due to the sheer massiveness of the rectangular retaining wall (Doyel 1974: 175-177). The present evidence suggests that most, if not all, of the mounds constructed in this manner were built during the Soho phase and were used into the Civano phase of the Classic period (Schroeder 1953; Doyel 1974, 1980; Gregory 1982).

Compound Walls

In addition to their manner of construction, another consistent feature of Classic period mounds is that in every known case but one, such mounds were surrounded by a rectangular compound wall. The only mound thought to lack such a feature is Mound 8 at Las Colinas, though there are grounds for arguing that a compound wall is present there, too. If the rectangular-retaining-wall form of platform mound is always accompanied by a surrounding rectangular compound wall, then the latter should be considered an element of platform mound morphology. Given the apparently consistent occurrence of palisades around the few earlier mounds that have been documented, the possibility that these palisades developed into the more substantial compound wall features of the Classic period should be considered. The proposed research at Las Colinas should establish whether or not a compound wall surrounded Mound 8 and thus determine the degree to which it conforms to the overall platform mound morphology described here.

The compound walls are less securely dated than the mounds themselves, but the regularity with which the two features occur together and the possible connection between the compound walls and the earlier palisades suggest that, in most cases, these features were probably built at the same time. The construction of the compound walls would thus also be principally Soho phase in date (Schroeder 1953: 178). If it is shown that a compound wall did indeed surround Mound 8, then it should be possible to determine the period of its construction and provide an additional test of the proposed Classic period origin of these walls.

Size and Orientation of Compounds

It has long been noted by various observers that platform mounds and their associated compound walls are oriented to the cardinal directions. Figure 1.2 illustrates the striking regularity with which the long axis of the compound has a north-south orientation. On that figure, the X-axis represents the north-south length of those compounds for which measurements are available, while the Y-axis represents their east-west dimension. The solid line in the middle is the dividing line between a north-south and an east-west orientation as determined by the long axis of the compound. The

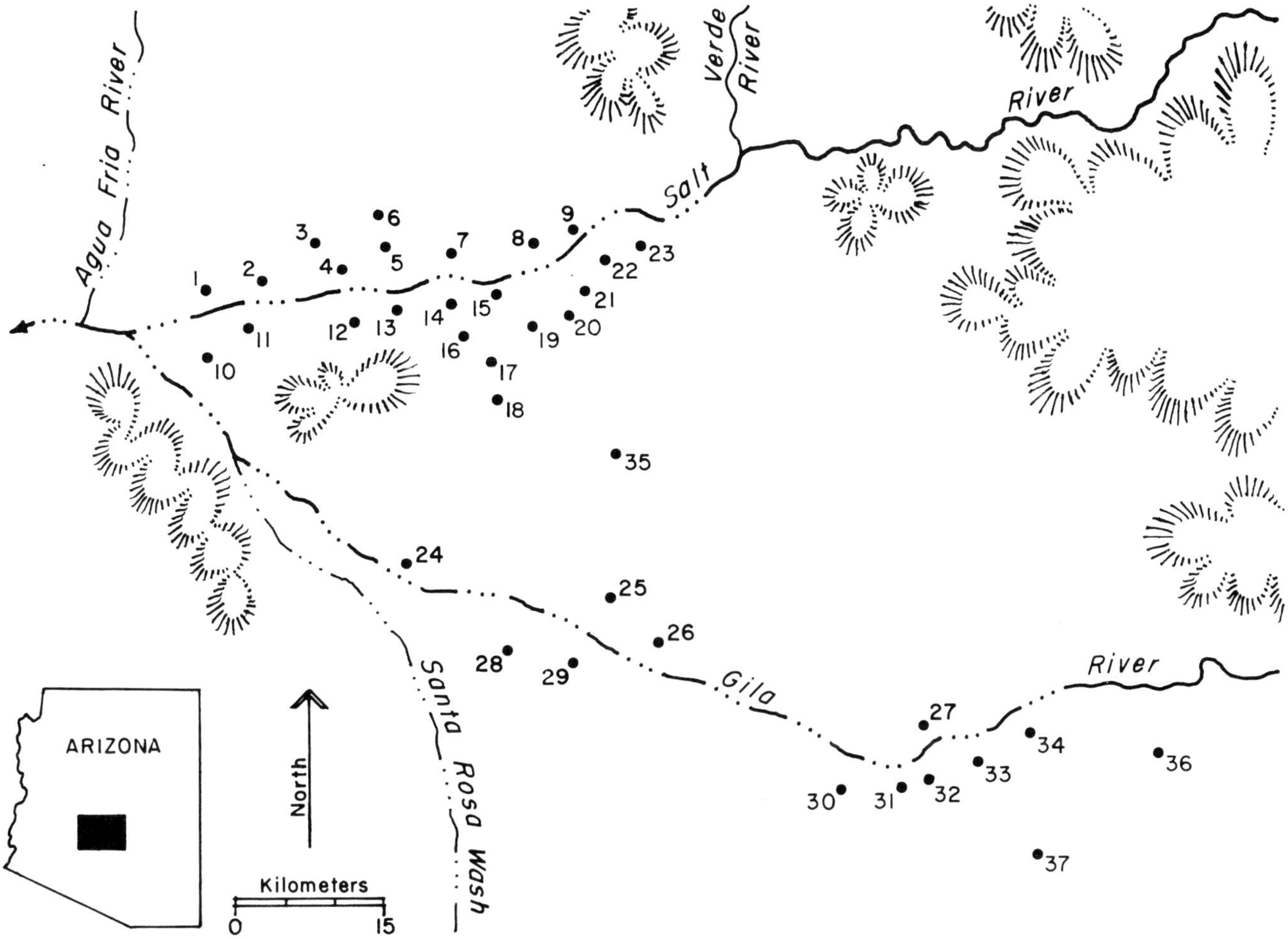

1 Pueblo del Alamo
2 Pueblo del Rio
3 Las Colinas
4 Casa Chica
5 La Ciudad
6 Casa Buena
7 Pueblo Grande
8 Pueblo Ultimo
9 Mesa 3:5 (Gila Pueblo), Compound A
10 Villa Buena
11 Pueblo Primero
12 Pueblo Viejo
13 Las Canopas
14 Pueblo del Monte
15 Plaza Tempe
16 Los Hornos
17 Los Guanacos
18 Los Muertos
19 Las Acequias
20 Casa de Mesa
21 Mesa Grande
22 El Caliche
23 Pueblo Moroni
24 Maricopa 3:2 (Gila Pueblo)
25 Lower Santan
26 Upper Santan
27 Escalante
28 Casa Blanca
29 Sweetwater
30 Casa Grande
31 Pueblo Bisnaga
32 Adamsville
33 Florence
34 Pueblo Pinal
35 Sonoqui Pueblo
36 Ruin 15 miles east of Florence
37 AZ AA:3:40 (ASM)

Figure 1.1 Platform mound sites in the Phoenix Basin.

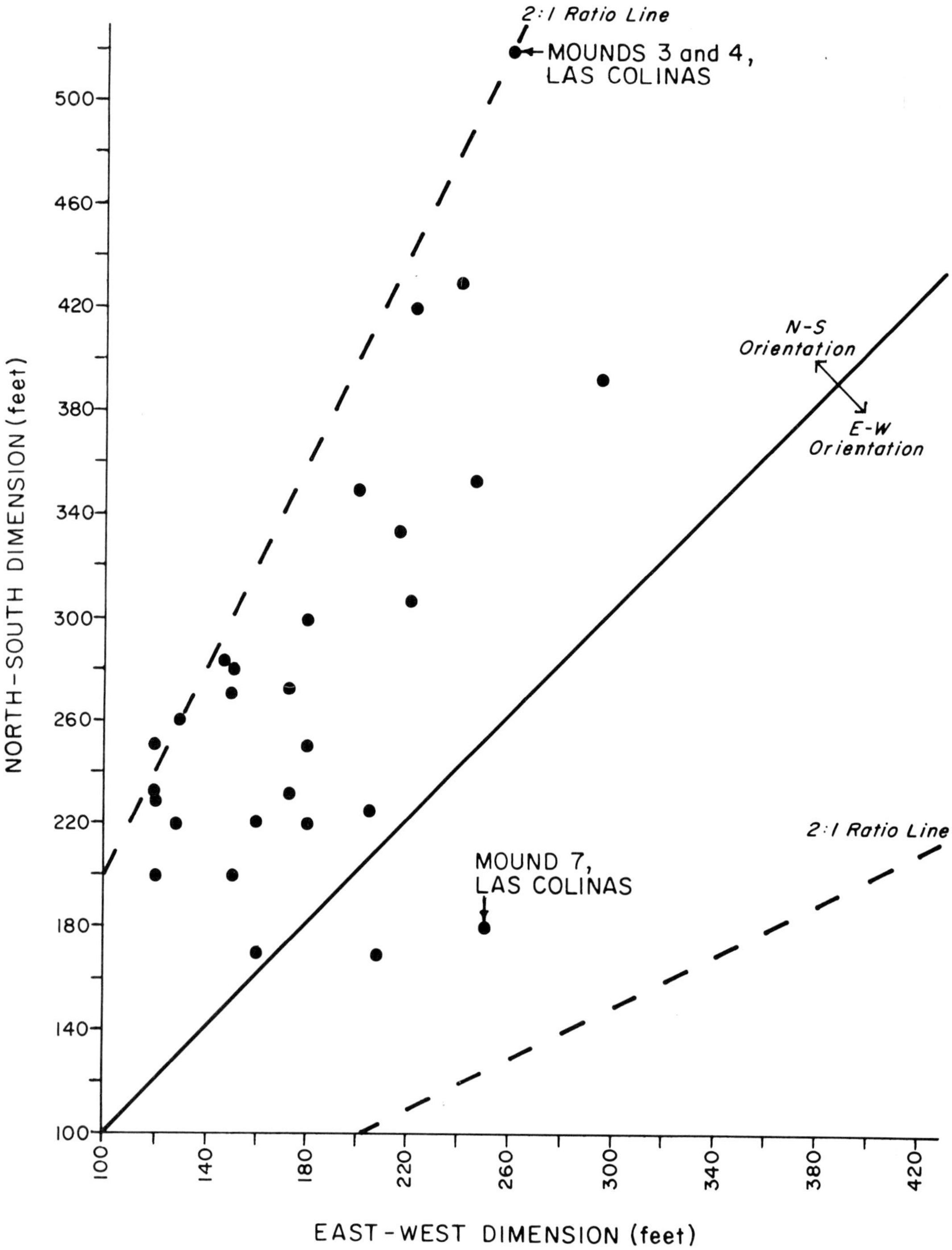

Figure 1.2. The size, shape, and orientation of compound walls around platform mounds.

two dotted lines represent the two-to-one ratio of the long and short axes, and each dot represents one compound. Clearly, a north-south orientation is the predominant pattern for this sample.

The size range of the compounds surrounding the platform mounds may also be seen in Figure 1.2. It shows essentially that there were a few very large ones, a few in the middle range, and many small ones. The dimensions of the compound walls surrounding platform mounds are the most consistently recorded measurements relating to this set of features; the sizes of the mounds themselves, in both the horizontal and vertical dimensions, are less frequently known. Recorded heights range from approximately 2.5 m to over 12 m, although these measurements are certainly affected by the date of observation and the degree to which a given mound had been leveled. In general, however, the available measurements suggest that both the height and lateral extent of the mounds within the compounds are roughly proportional to the size of the surrounding enclosure. Thus, Figure 1.2 also represents the approximate relative size of the mounds contained within the respective compounds. The largest compound recorded was at Las Colinas, around Mounds 3 and 4, and another, medium-sized, compound wall was constructed around Mound 7.

Placement of Mounds Within Compounds

The placement of the mounds within their respective compounds was apparently quite regular. With minor variations, there are two consistently occurring positions shown in Figure 1.3. An idealized representation of both patterns is shown, with the names of the sites having that placement listed next to the representation. The most commonly occurring position is in the western part of the compound, with the west retaining wall of the mound either abutting or very close to the compound wall. Most of the mounds featuring this placement are roughly centered or slightly south of center along the western wall of the compound. The Escalante mound, placed in the very northwestern corner of the compound, represents a variation on the western position. Several examples of a north-central placement are known, represented by the mounds at Los Muertos, Casa Blanca, and possibly Plaza Tempe. The Sweetwater mound is somewhat similarly placed, although Fewkes shows it more or less in the center of its associated compound enclosure (Fewkes 1908: 320).

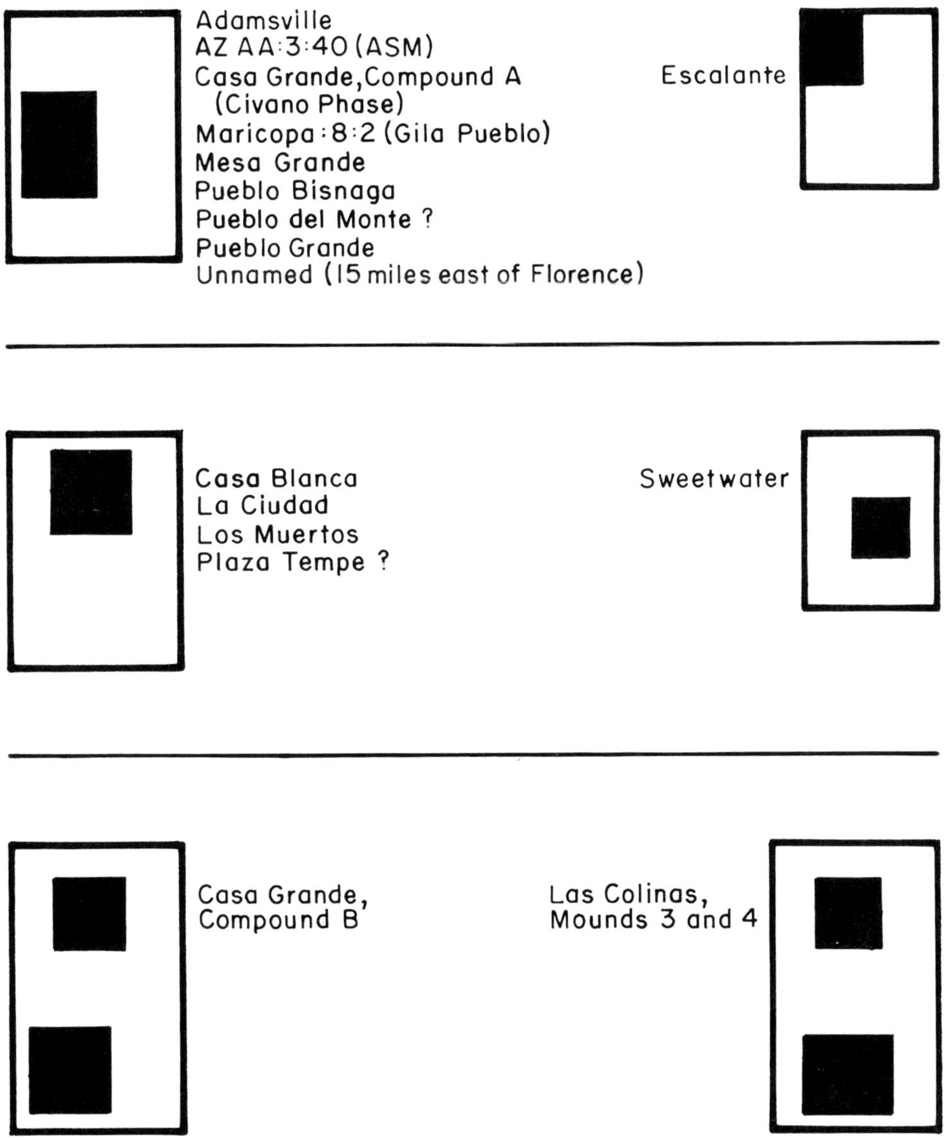

Figure 1.3. The position of mounds within compounds.

In the only two compounds which contain two platform mounds, at the sites of Casa Grande and Las Colinas, the placement of the two mounds is similar.

Because only 17 mounds can be plotted with respect to their position within the compound wall, little more can be said concerning this aspect of patterning. The available data suggest that the placement of mounds within compounds was not arbitrary, but tended to be, with minor variations, in a western or north-central position.

Features on the Mounds and within the Compounds

An important feature of platform mounds and their associated compounds is that pit house-type structures, caliche-walled rooms, and a variety of other features were built on the mounds and within the confines of the compound walls. At those sites for which data are available, such as Las Colinas, Pueblo Grande, Mesa Grande, Los Muertos, Casa Grande, and Escalante, a complex sequence of construction and superposition is indicated. Consistent with the dating of the mounds and compounds themselves, this sequence of construction seems in every case to have begun during the Soho phase and continued into the Civano phase.

No systematic study of the changing spatial relations represented in these construction sequences has yet been undertaken, and very few of the relevant data are available in published form; nor do we yet have comparative analyses of the differential distribution of artifact classes recovered from structures and other features on mounds and within compounds. To the degree that such investigations could be accomplished with the existing data, they would provide the basis for a variety of inferences concerning the size and character of the social groups who were housed in those constructions, the specific kinds of activities carried out on the mounds and within the compounds, and the changes in these variables that may have occurred during the occupation of specific sites.

Classic Period Site Structure

In addition to the above-noted regularities in the morphology of platform mounds and their associated compounds, there is evidence of a consistently structured relationship between these features and other constructions within the same sites. Although ballcourts are the most notable of these features, large compounds without platform mounds, and possibly large roomblocks without compound walls, may also be considered basic elements in this structure. Smaller roomblocks, trash mounds, cremation areas, hornos, and other smaller features have not been considered in the present discussion, owing primarily to the lack of data concerning their locations within particular sites. The distribution of these less obtrusive features may well provide another dimension to the rather basic structure described here, and it is my suspicion that, were sufficient data available, their inclusion would further refine the patterning now discussed.

The postulated site structure may be best illustrated with reference to maps of those sites where relatively complete information is available concerning the locations of at least the principal constructions. In Figures 1.4 and 1.5, platform mounds and their associated compounds, ballcourts, and other major constructions at several Classic period sites are shown as separate symbols. Note that, at La Cuidad (Fig. 1.4), the combination of the platform mound and other major constructions forms the area within which the ballcourt is contained, and which contains no other features; this structure is duplicated at Casa Grande (Fig. 1.4). The maps of Villa Buena and Pueblo Viejo illustrate this pattern to some degree, as do those of Casa de Mesa, Pueblo Grande, Adamsville, Lower Santan, and El Caliche (Fig. 1.5). The scale of the pattern is much increased at Las Colinas (Fig. 1.4) and there are multiple platform mounds, one of which (Mound 8) is closely associated with the ballcourt; nonetheless, the basic pattern is again repeated.

The most often recorded—and thus preserved—aspect of the proposed Classic period site structure is the location of the ballcourt relative to the platform mounds and associated compounds. Ballcourts are known to have existed at 23 of the 37 sites considered here, and only Los Muertos and Escalante may be confidently said to have lacked courts. The data from the remaining 12 sites are not sufficient to determine whether or not courts were present.

The position of the ballcourt relative to the platform mound is known for 17 of the 23 sites where courts have been documented. Figure 1.6 illustrates the degree of regularity in the positioning of the courts at these sites. An idealized platform mound and compound is shown with north-south and east-west axes passing through the center of the features and thus dividing the surrounding space into four quadrants. The names of sites with ballcourts are shown in the quadrant in which their respective ballcourts lie.

It is clear that the majority of courts were in the northeast quadrant with respect to the platform mound; within this quadrant, the position of a ballcourt may range from almost due north to due east. Several sites have more than one ballcourt and two sites have more than one platform mound, so that there is in these cases more than one position recorded for the ballcourt. Interestingly, two of the five sites where the ballcourt lies in other than the northeast quadrant are those with multiple platform mounds and the northeast position of the court holds for at least one of the mounds. At another of these sites, Pueblo Grande, the ballcourt is within the northwest quadrant, but lies very close to the north-south line; thus its position is similar to that seen in the majority of the sites.

This patterning in site structure has several implications. First, despite minor variations, these data suggest that there existed a shared and consistent conception of the proper layout of platform mounds, ballcourts, and associated features within sites. Second, these sets of features appear to define a central site area in each of the sites, possibly including one or more plazas associated with the features. Finally, the consistent association of ballcourts with platform mounds suggests that the courts may have been in use well into the Classic period and that some courts may even have been built during the Classic period.

Summary

This brief analysis shows: (1) that Las Colinas was 1 of 38 known Classic period Hohokam sites in the Phoenix Basin which had features known as platform mounds; (2) that Las Colinas had the most platform mounds (four) of any known Classic period site and it is one of only two sites known to have had more than one mound; (3) that two of the mounds at Las Colinas were enclosed within a compound wall that is the largest yet recorded; and (4) that platform mound sites exhibit regularity in the arrangement of features within them, and Las Colinas shows a pattern similar to that seen at other platform mound sites.

Evidence for a Preclassic Period Occupation at Las Colinas

While it is clear that Las Colinas was a major Classic period site, its size and relative importance during the Preclassic periods are largely unknown. Several lines of evidence suggest that there was a substantial Preclassic occupation and that this occupation may have occurred primarily during the Sacaton phase of the Sedentary period. The presence of a Sedentary period component is important to several of the research problems outlined in Chapter 2, particularly those dealing with various aspects of the transition from the Sedentary to the Classic period.

During the 1968 excavations at Mound 8, portions of a pit house floor (Feature 120) were exposed in a trench through the east side of the mound (Hammack 1981: 59). On the basis of a single sherd of Santa Cruz Red-on-buff, this structure was tentatively assigned to the Santa Cruz phase. Another pit house (Feature 112) lying to the west of the mound was assigned a Sacaton phase date solely on the basis of architectural style and stratigraphic position (Hammack and Sullivan 1981: 41). This house was intruded through a trash deposit, so that if the Sacaton phase assignment for the house is correct, there were already earlier trash deposits in place at the time of its construction. Further evidence of a Sacaton phase occupation of the general area is provided by the decorated ceramic assemblages recovered from the fill of the internal cells of Mound 8 itself. These assemblages were composed of 13 to 56 percent Sacaton Red-on-buff, accompanied by from 31 to 85 percent Casa Grande Red-on-buff, the latter often exhibiting Santan Red-on-buff design elements (Crown 1981a). These findings are consonant with an early Soho phase starting date for the construction of the mound, and also suggest that Sacaton phase trash deposits contributed to the fill of the mound. The large numbers of Sacaton Red-on-buff sherds indicate that a substantial amount of trash is represented, and it is likely that the Sacaton phase trash deposits that contributed to the fill of Mound 8, as well as the structures that housed the groups who produced this trash, were located somewhere in the general vicinity of the mound.

There is indirect evidence from the 1968 excavations for a possible Sacaton feature or features (nonhouse) in the immediate area of Mound 8. First, the massive, post-reinforced "Wall A" at the core of the initial mound construction, appears to have been truncated by two of the lighter, post-reinforced walls that formed the central retaining cells (Fig. 1.7). As Hammack suggests, this wall may have been part of an earlier construction that was razed when Mound 8 was built. This construction is of unknown form and may date to the Sacaton phase (Hammack 1981). It is of some interest that this truncated wall is quite similar to the wall that formed the retaining wall for Stage III construction at the Gatlin mound (Wasley 1960, Fig. 5), a feature which was constructed and enlarged numerous times during the Sacaton phase. In addition to this massive wall, there is a long, post-reinforced wall—clearly not a house wall—which extends under all of the walls that are part of the Mound 8 construction sequence (Hammack and Sullivan 1981, Map 1). It therefore predates construction of the mound on the basis of stratigraphic relationships, and represents a possible Sedentary period feature (Hammack and Sullivan 1981: 20, 60). If Hammack's early Soho phase date for the construction of Stage III of Mound 8 is correct, then this post-reinforced wall probably dates to the Sacaton phase. These data are discussed in greater detail below.

The recent testing program also provides some evidence for a Sacaton phase occupation in areas away from Mound 8. Although the total number of decorated sherds recovered was small (n=137), 25 sherds of Sacaton Red-on-buff were counted in the sample, a number equaled or surpassed only by Santa Cruz Red-on-buff (n=25) and Gila Polychrome (n=32). Sacaton Red-on-buff was most frequent in Areas 4 (n=10) and 5 (n=11), but also occurred in Area 1 (n=4). The Santa Cruz Red-on-buff sherds recovered were concentrated in Area 1, suggesting that Santa Cruz phase material is concentrated far to the east of Mound 8; however, this area may also contain Sacaton phase materials. Most Sacaton phase material appears to be concentrated in Areas 4 and 5, to the west of the mound. Because some of these sherds were recovered from trash pits (Schreiber and others 1981), there must have been a Sacaton phase occupation to produce the refuse.

In summary, there is a substantial amount of evidence to show that a Preclassic occupation existed at Las Colinas within the corridor area. This occupation appears to be represented primarily by Sacaton phase materials, although

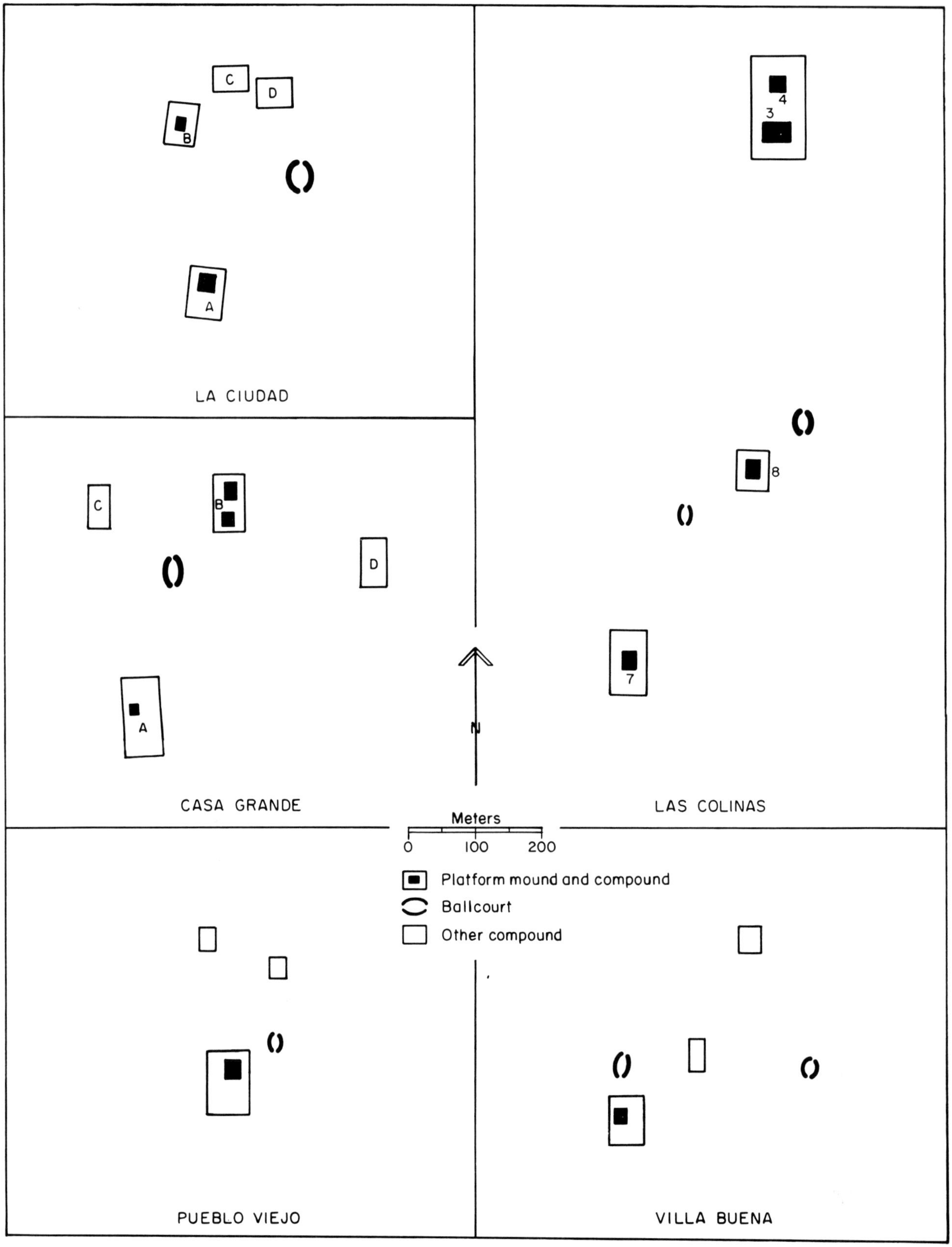

Figure 1.4. The layout of compounds, platform mounds, and ballcourts at La Ciudad, Casa Grande, Pueblo Viejo, Villa Buena, and Las Colinas.

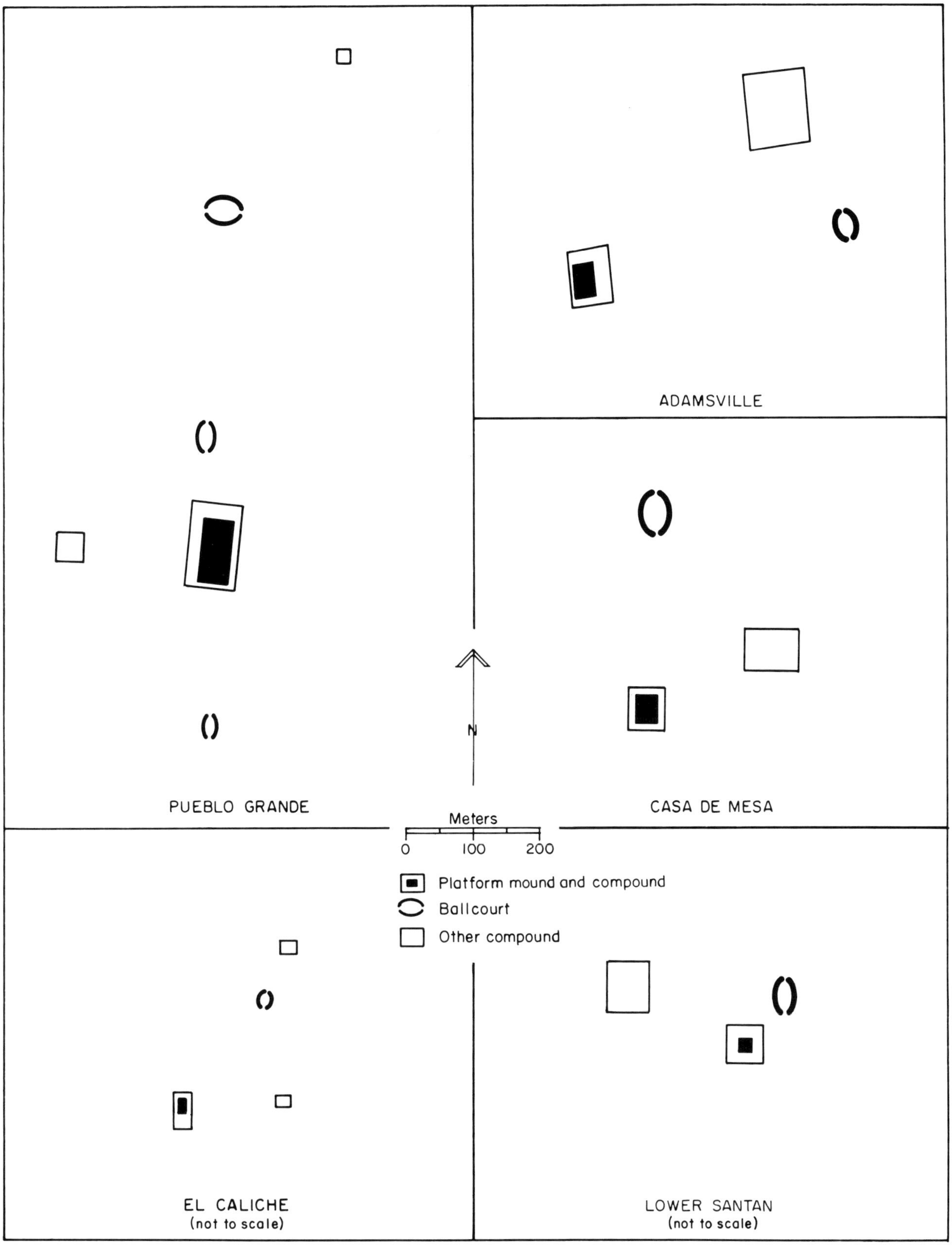

Figure 1.3. The layout of compounds, platform mounds, and ballcourts at Casa de Mesa, Adamsville, Pueblo Grande, El Caliche, and Lower Santan.

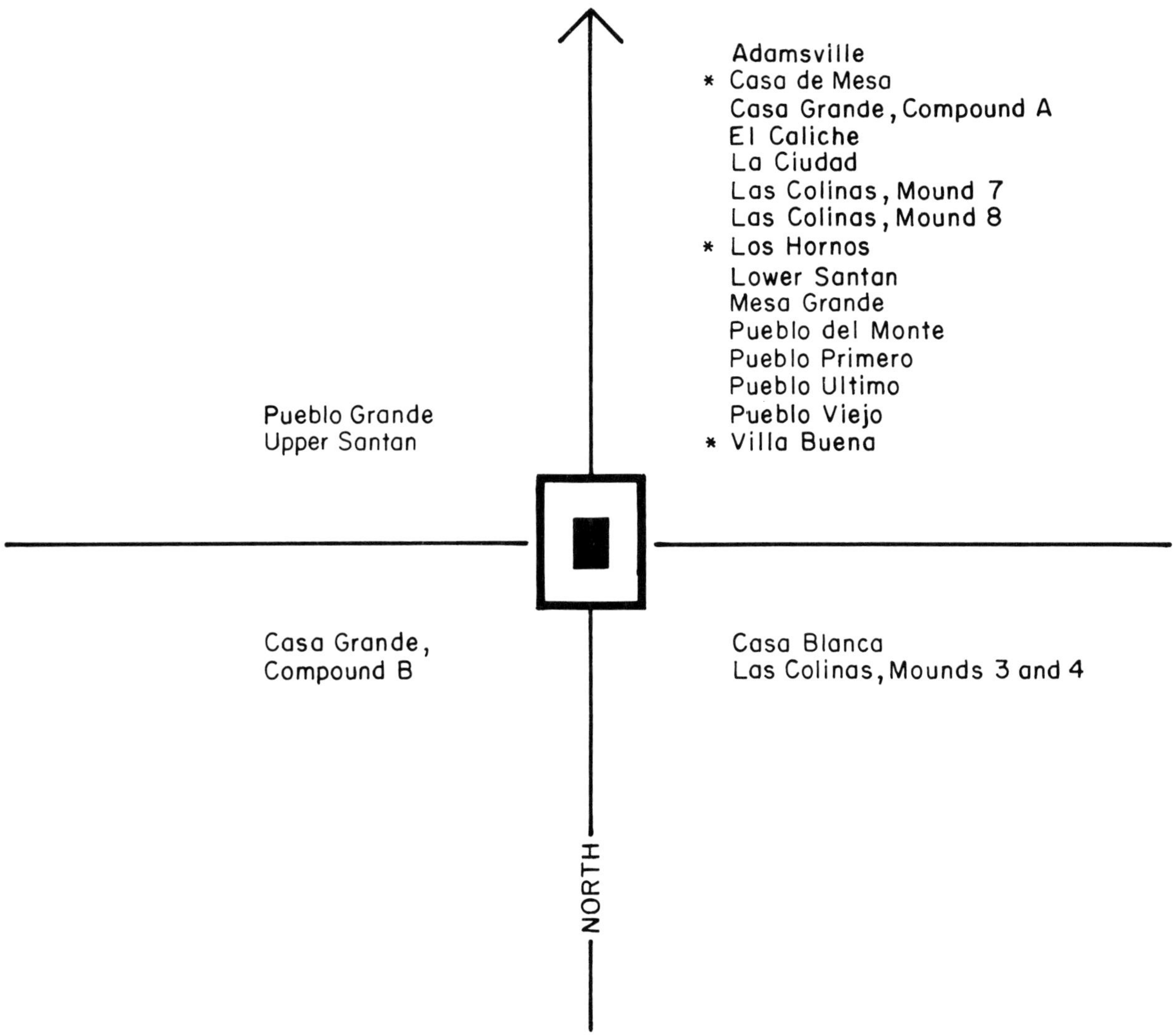

Figure 1.6. The position of ballcourts relative to platform mounds. An asterisk (*) indicates sites with two or more ballcourts.

there is some evidence to suggest a concentration of Santa Cruz phase material in Area 1, well to the east of Mound 8, and the possibility of Santa Cruz phase features beneath and south of Mound 8 cannot be discounted. We may expect to find a substantial amount of Preclassic material and associated features, presenting the opportunity to study the Preclassic period occupation of the site. With the exception of a few sherds of Gila Butte Red-on-buff from the fill of Mound 8, there is no evidence for occupation of the site prior to the Santa Cruz phase of the Colonial period (A.D. 700-900).

Finally, although the ballcourt reported to be east of Mound 8 was not located during the 1968 excavations, there is reason to believe that it did exist and may be discovered by further exploration (see the discussion of Corridor Area 2 below). Present evidence suggests that most Hohokam ballcourts were built during the Sedentary period, although there is a growing body of data which supports a Classic period construction date for at least some of these features (Wilcox and Sternberg 1983). Thus the discovery and dating of this feature will be an important goal of the research, and if the feature proves to be Sacaton in date, it would constitute a significant feature of the Preclassic occupation of the site.

The Nature of the Sample Defined by the Freeway Corridor

In the course of developing the research design for the now-completed testing program at Las Colinas, a map was prepared showing the distribution of all known surface and subsurface features and deposits at the site (Gregory and McGuire 1982; Schreiber and others 1981). The data recovered during the testing program have been used to up date that map, as shown in Figure 1.8. The nature of the materials in the freeway corridor is summarized here by corridor area, and additional information regarding the nature

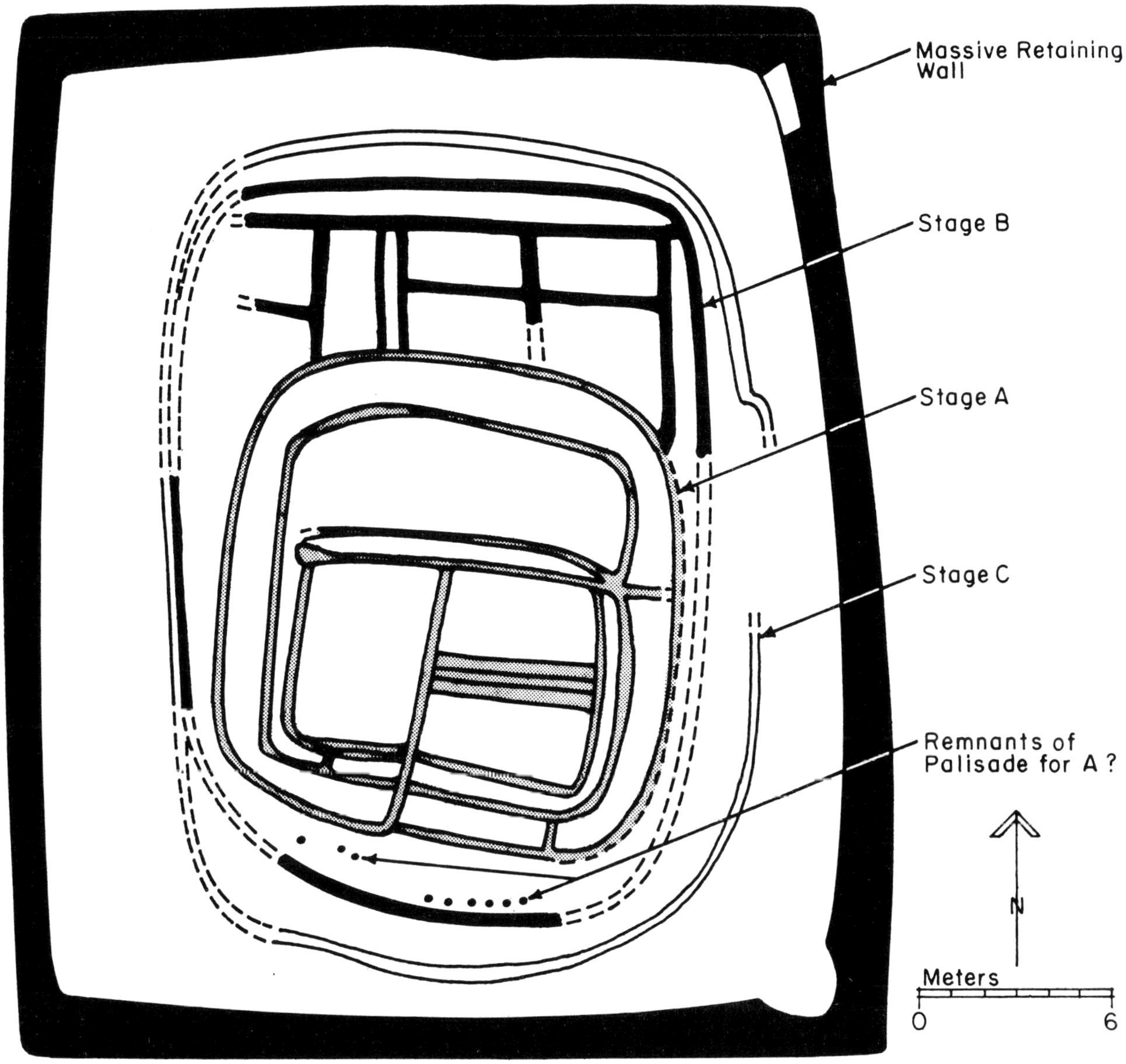

Figure 1.7. Construction stages at Mound 8, Las Colinas (Hammack and Sullivan 1981).

of the sample is presented. In general, the expectations delineated in the testing research design with respect to general site stratigraphy and the distribution of subsurface features and deposits were confirmed by the testing.

Area 1

Thirteen prehistoric features were discovered in this area during the testing, including three canal segments (Schreiber and others 1981: 79). One of the canal segments appears to be part of the large Canal Number 5, or Canal Colinas (Turney 1929). The other 10 features include an inhumation, a cremation, 2 charcoal lenses, 3 trash pits, and 3 other pits. With the exception of the canal segments and one of the pits, most of these features are clustered in the western end of this area. One of the trash pits produced Classic period material, but most of the ceramics recovered from the remaining features indicate that a Preclassic period occupation is represented. Although no structures were encountered, the presence of the trash pits, as well as a cremation and an inhumation, makes it likely that one or more habitation areas are represented, and that the remains of one or more structures are present.

Area 2

No features were encountered in Corridor Area 2 during the testing. Combined with the few features recorded in this area during the 1968 excavations, these findings indicate that the overall feature density in Area 2 is low.

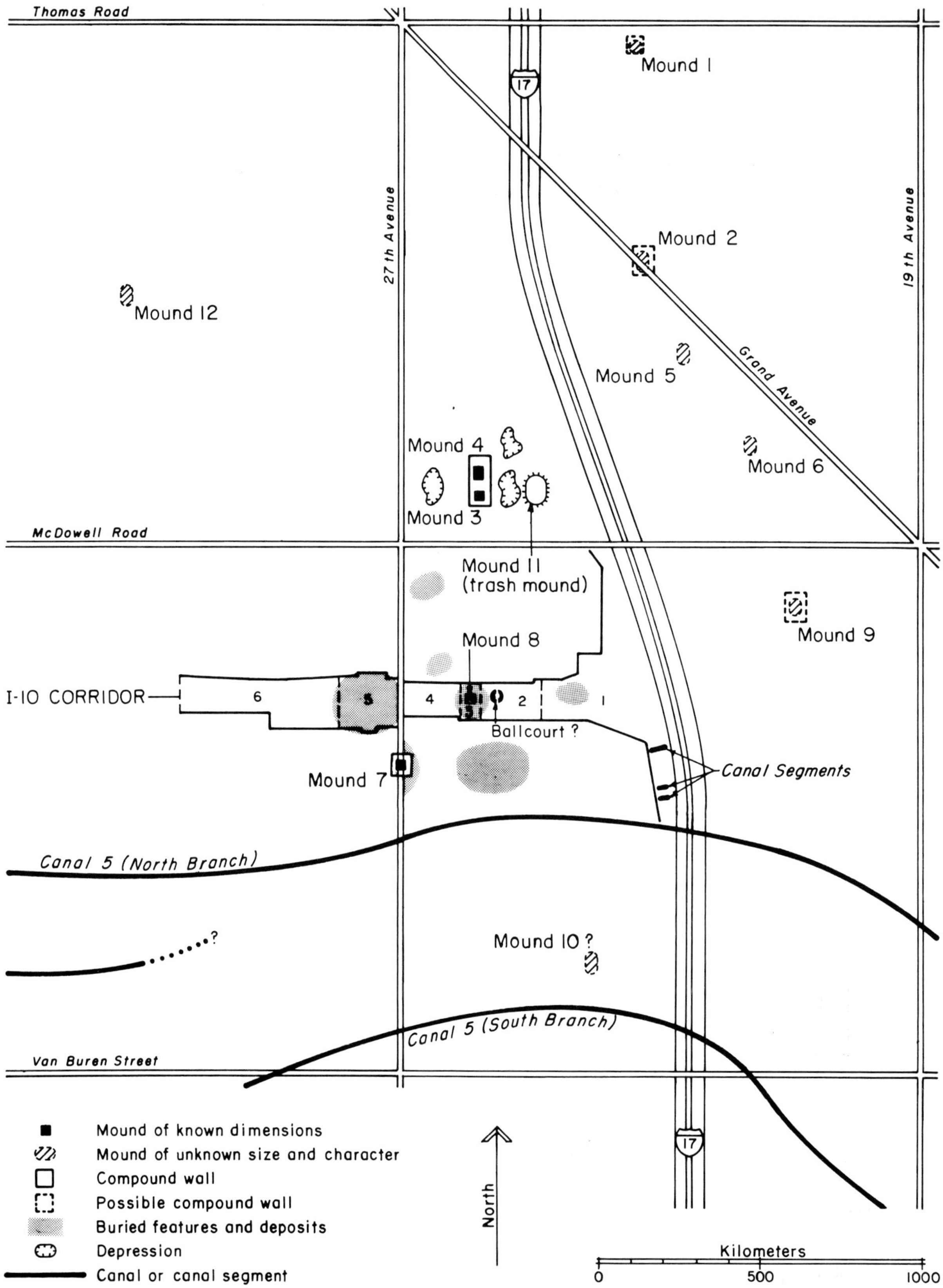

Figure 1.8. Distribution of features at Las Colinas.

The trenches excavated in this area in 1968 were part of an ultimately futile search for the ballcourt reported by Turney (1929) in this general area. It is, presumably, the same court seen by Pinart in 1876, prior to the beginning of cultivation (Pinart 1962). The failure to find the ballcourt appears at first to be puzzling, because Turney was usually accurate in the relative placement of features within sites included on his maps (Turney 1929; Wilcox and Sternberg 1983). Two possibilities exist: either the ballcourt was not located anywhere in the area now defined by the freeway corridor, or the remains of the ballcourt are present and have not yet been discovered. Figure 1.10 makes it clear that the ballcourt could have gone undiscovered, despite the level of trenching accomplished in this area. The size of the hypothetical ballcourt shown in various positions in this figure is based on an average of ballcourt sizes compiled in a recent study of these features by Wilcox (Wilcox and Sternberg 1983). That portions of a ballcourt can be preserved despite the effects of cultivation, and also be invisible on the surface, was shown by recent excavations at Los Hornos. According to David Wilcox, the fill and lower floors of a ballcourt were discovered at that site below a 40-cm-thick plow zone.

Determining whether there was indeed a ballcourt in Area 2 will be important to a number of the research questions to be addressed at the site. For the moment, it is sufficient to note the possibility that the remains of the ballcourt still exist, as illustrated by the foregoing discussion and accompanying figure. It is also probable that additional cremations may be present in the area.

Area 3

This area includes the feature known as Mound 8 and the area immediately surrounding it. It has been demonstrated that Corridor Area 3 is essentially the same as the yard of the house which once sat atop Mound 8, and that this is the only area of the corridor which has never been plowed (Gregory and McGuire 1982). Mound 8 was the focus of intensive excavations in 1968, and a final report on that work has now been published (Hammack and Sullivan 1981). Those investigations revealed a small platform mound which had undergone a complex sequence of enlargement and rebuilding, and an equally complex sequence of structures occupying the areas around the mound, especially to the west (Hammack 1981, Figs. 8, 14, and 15; Hammack and Sullivan 1981, Map 1). The construction of the mound and associated features occurred primarily during the Soho and Civano phases of the Classic period, although as noted above, at least two Preclassic structures were recorded.

It is not necessary to review in detail the information contained in the extensive report on this mound and the immediately surrounding areas; however, several points are relevant to the research proposed at the site. First, it is clear from the map of the site that not all of the mound was excavated (Hammack and Sullivan 1981, Map 1). Although the bulk of the fill of the mound was removed during the excavations, and some of the walls were later pushed down for safety reasons, some small portions of the fill remain, as do the profile cuts through the mound (for example, the areas between Features 16 and 75, 63 and 73, and 45 and 88, and the profiles at the west side of Feature 57 and between Features 2 and 4). In addition, several features were not completely excavated, including a Preclassic pit house lying beneath the mound (Feature 120), a Soho phase pit house at the west side of the mound (Feature 125), and a Civano phase structure at the western edge of the excavated area (Feature 39).

Second, the area south of the mound, where the backdirt from the excavations was placed, was not intensively investigated. Hammack (1969: 12) notes:

> Dirt was removed by wheelbarrow and placed in large dump piles to the south. A few archaeological features may have been covered by this process. However, prior extensive testing in the dump pile areas yielded little indication of prehistoric usage.

However, an exhaustive review of the photographic record and the field notes from the project has produced no evidence of backhoe trenches other than those which may be seen on the aerial photograph shown in the site report and which are also shown in Figure 1.9. Therefore, we do not know where the trenches were placed nor how many of them there were; this is also true of the narrow strip north of the excavated areas and immediately south of the northern margin of the corridor. Even if the trenches were dug at approximately the same interval as in Area 2, numerous features and deposits may have gone undetected.

Finally, except for a discussion of the sequence of mound construction and the dating of the structures associated with the mound, the complex sequence of use of the space defined by Mound 8 and adjacent areas is essentially uninterpreted. It is not clear exactly which structures were present in relation to which episode of mound construction; it is thus difficult to address questions about the degree of formality which may be present in the use of space, the size and makeup of the social groups which occupied these areas, and so on. Given the series of archaeomagnetic dates obtained during the 1968 excavations as well as the stratigraphic relationships between features, a reconstruction of the use of space in the mound area *would* be possible and is important to an understanding of a variety of problems dealing with the function and development of the mound.

In summary, it is likely that features are present to the south, west, and possibly north of Mound 8, in areas which were unexcavated or tested at an unknown level of intensity in 1968. Partially unexcavated features remain beneath and west of the mound, and several small portions of the mound fill, as well as profile cuts, remain intact. The sequence of construction documented for the mound and the areas immediately surrounding it remains essentially uninterpreted, especially with respect to both the changes which occurred through time in the use of the surrounding space, and the

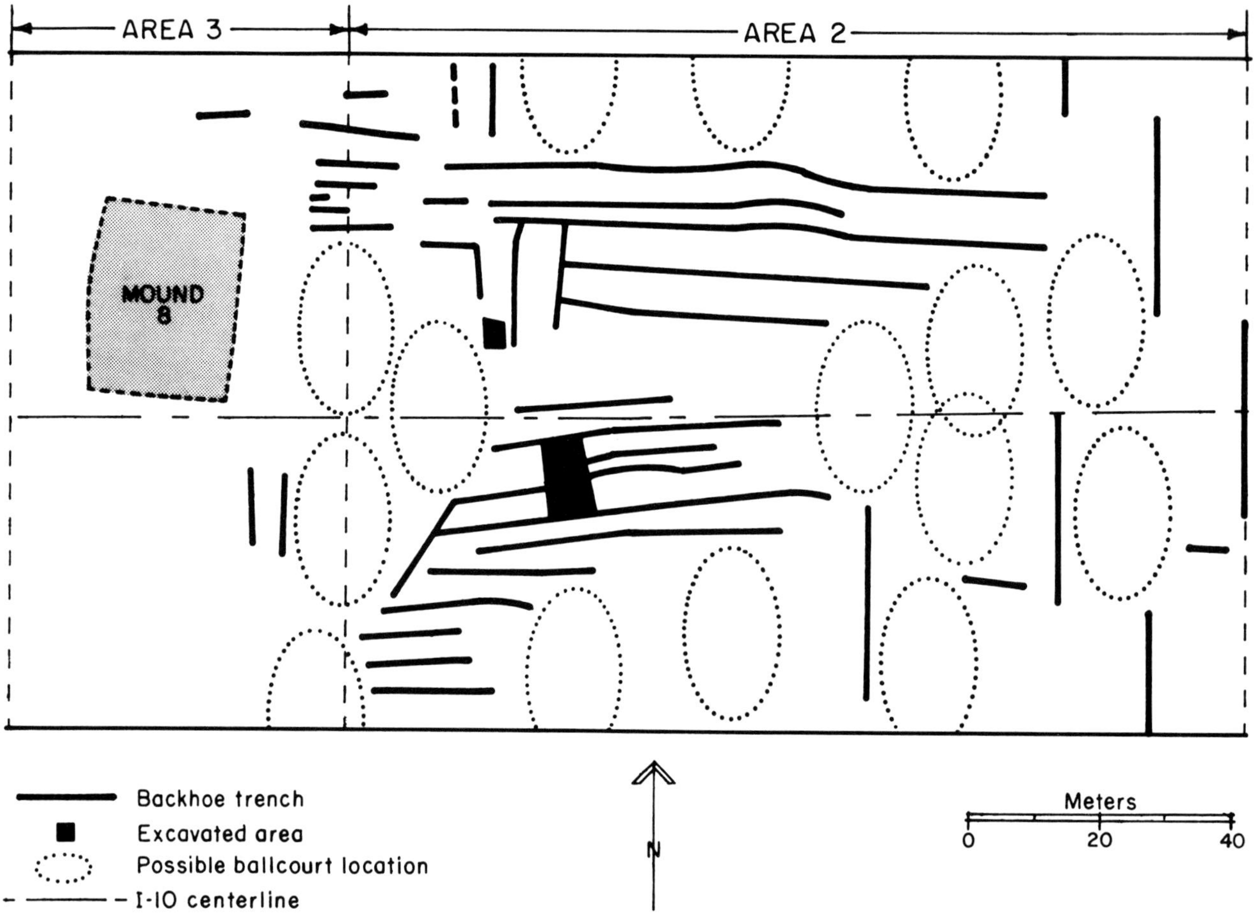

Figure 1.9. Map of Corridor Areas 2 and 3, showing the locations of previous test trenches and hand excavations, and possible positions of the ballcourt.

size and composition of the social groups represented. Therefore, a considerable amount of information that will be important to a number of the research problems defined for the site remains to be collected in Area 3.

Area 4

Only two trenches were placed in the very western end of Area 4 during the testing program. When features were encountered in both of these trenches, the testing of this area was discontinued, as dictated by the research design (Gregory and McGuire 1982; Schreiber and others 1981). The features included a very large trash pit, a smaller trash pit, and what appears to be a trash-filled pit house. Although the dating of these features is not certain, it appears that the trash pits may represent mixed Classic period and Preclassic deposits, while the single pit house may be Classic period in date.

While the remainder of this area was not tested, it is likely that a high density of features and deposits is present. This conclusion is based on the following observations:

1. The distribution of features between Areas 4 and 5 appears to have been continuous.

2. Part of the unplowed area which formed the yard of the house formerly atop Mound 8 extends into the eastern end of Area 4 and is visible as a slight rise in that area; the unexcavated portion of at least one of the features discovered in 1968 (Feature 39) lies in this area and alignments of vegetation typically indicative of caliche walls have been observed here.

3. Subsurface deposits have been reported immediately to the north of Corridor Area 4, uncovered when the foundations for the buildings now in that area were excavated (Gregory and McGuire 1982).

4. The proximity of the area to Mound 8 makes it likely on logical grounds and by comparison with other sites (for example, Pueblo Grande) that this general area was a focus of occupation through at least the Classic period and perhaps during the Preclassic as well.

Area 5

Area 5 produced the highest density of features encountered during the testing program. Five pits, one pit house, one hearth, two possible occupation surfaces, and one inhumation were recorded (Schreiber and others 1981: 105). Although relatively few diagnostic ceramics were recovered, it appears that both Classic period and Preclassic occupations are represented. This was the only area in which possible extramural occupation surfaces were recorded, suggesting that cultivation may not have reached the same depth or produced the same degree of disturbance as in the other areas.

The discovery of a high density of features in Area 5 tends to confirm reports that buried features and deposits were encountered when sewer trenches were dug along 27th Avenue (Gregory and McGuire 1982), and combined with the features encountered in the western end of Area 4, would indicate a continuous distribution of features between the two areas.

Area 6

Only a very small portion of the western end of Corridor Area 6 was available for testing, and nothing is known about the distribution of subsurface features and deposits in the remainder of the area. The minimal surface remains recorded by the original survey of the corridor would indicate a low feature density; however, the discovery during testing of a number of features in Area 1, which had a similar surface artifact density, dictates that caution be exercised in assessing the untested portions of Area 6. This is especially true of the eastern end of the area, which is contiguous with Area 5, where a high density of features was recorded.

Additional Considerations

Several additional points may be made, creating a broader conception of the available sample of the site of Las Colinas.

First, an area of similar size and shape may be imposed on maps of other Classic period sites having platform mounds. Disregarding for the moment the flaring of the corridor at the eastern end of the site area and the minor variations in shape which occur elsewhere, the corridor is essentially a ribbonlike swath with a width of approximately 100 m, running from east to west through the site area. The reported location of the ballcourt is within its path, as is Mound 8 (Fig. 1.10). Figures 1.10 and 1.11 show the hypothetical placement of similar corridors across maps of other Classic period sites having platform mounds and ballcourts; these figures show the general character of the sample that would be obtained if the freeway corridor made its way through these sites. Given the foregoing discussion of the structure of Classic period Hohokam sites with platform mounds, these figures illustrate the proposition that the corridor segment through Las Colinas cuts what was probably part of the central site area, as would be the case if such a corridor cut through any of the other sites illustrated here.

Despite the shared identity of these sites as members of a class of sites having platform mounds and ballcourts, and the general similarities in site structure already pointed out, it would be a mistake to suggest that transects placed through each of these sites would produce comparable samples. Therefore, caution must be exercised in generalizing the results of the proposed data collection at Las Colinas. Because the overall distribution of features at Las Colinas, as well as the spacing of the platform mounds and the ballcourt, is on a larger scale than at any of the other sites, a similar transect at another site would produce a larger spatial sample of the central site area (as defined by the axis between the largest architectural features) than will the transect at Las Colinas. While it is difficult to assess the significance of these differences in scale at the present time, they should be kept in mind when interpreting the data recovered from Las Colinas and when selecting comparative data for subsequent analyses.

If we assume for the moment that the entire corridor segment under consideration would be included within the site boundaries, and assume as well that the former acreage of the site falls within the rough estimates previously described (1.3 to 1.9 square miles), then the area of the corridor represents between 3.2 and 4.6 percent of the total site area. Because the western boundary of the site area probably falls within Corridor Area 6, and because much of the northern part of Area 1 is essentially removed from consideration, this figure should be reduced accordingly. Although these estimates are very rough, they do give some idea of the portion of the site represented by the corridor segment, and provide a general conception of the size of the present sample relative to the total former extent of the site.

It should be apparent from Figures 1.10 and 1.11 that this is a much smaller proportion of the site than would be represented by a similar segment through other Classic period platform mound sites, at least with respect to the central area of the site as defined by the distribution of platform mounds, ballcourts, and other major architectural features.

Summary

The background information presented here shows that Las Colinas was one of the largest Classic period Hohokam sites in the Phoenix Basin, and that it is further distinguished by the fact that at least four platform mounds were built at the site, all of which were in use simultaneously for some time during the Classic period. The compound wall which surrounded Mounds 3 and 4 is the largest such feature yet documented at a Hohokam site. Furthermore, Las Colinas exhibits an arrangement of features which parallels that seen at other Classic period sites with platform mounds, but on a much larger scale than at other sites.

There is substantial evidence for a Preclassic occupation of the site, which may have been extensive during the Sacaton

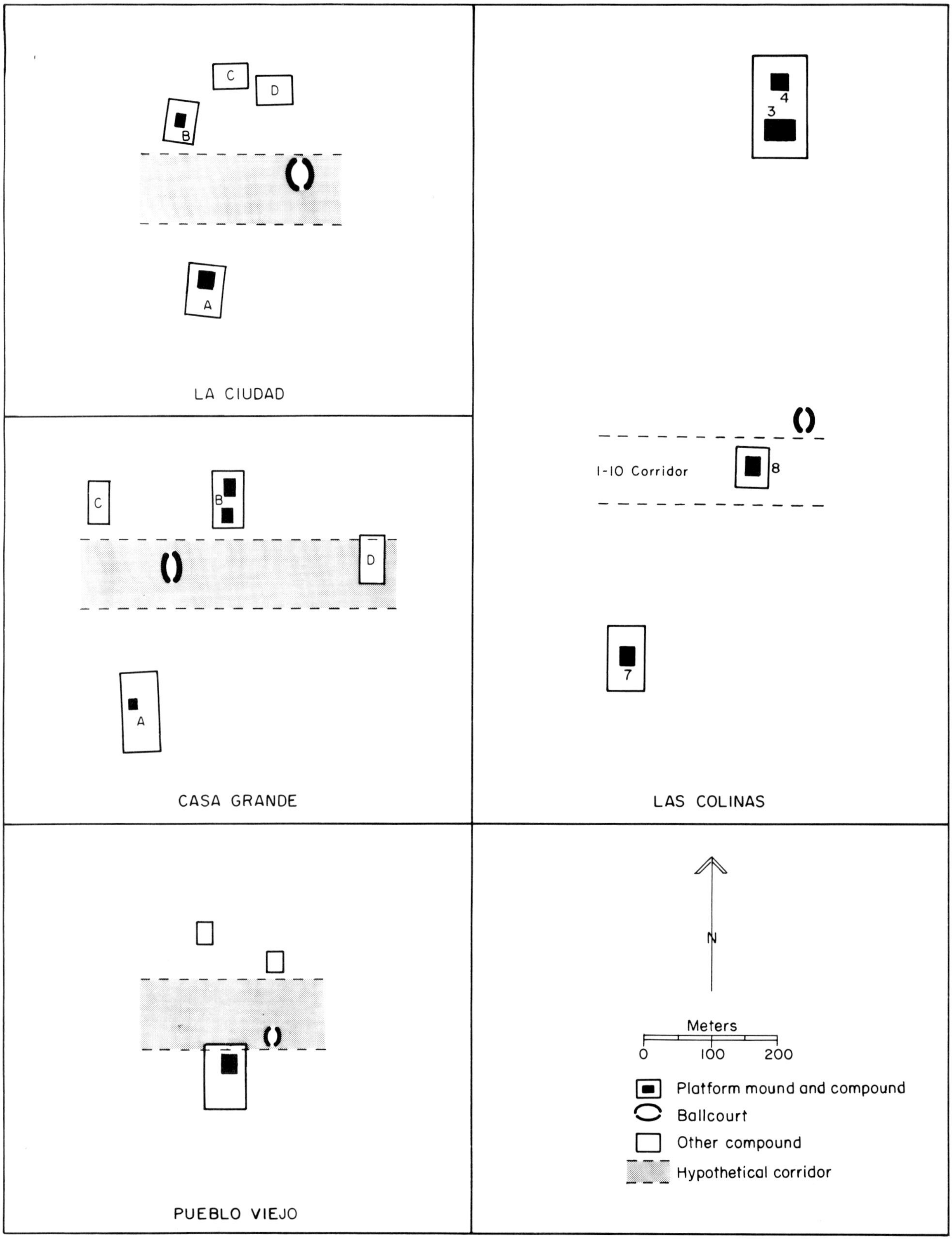

Figure 1.10. The location of the I-10 freeway corridor relative to platform mounds, compounds, and the ballcourt at Las Colinas, and locations of hypothetical corridors across La Cuidad, Casa Grande, and Pueblo Viejo.

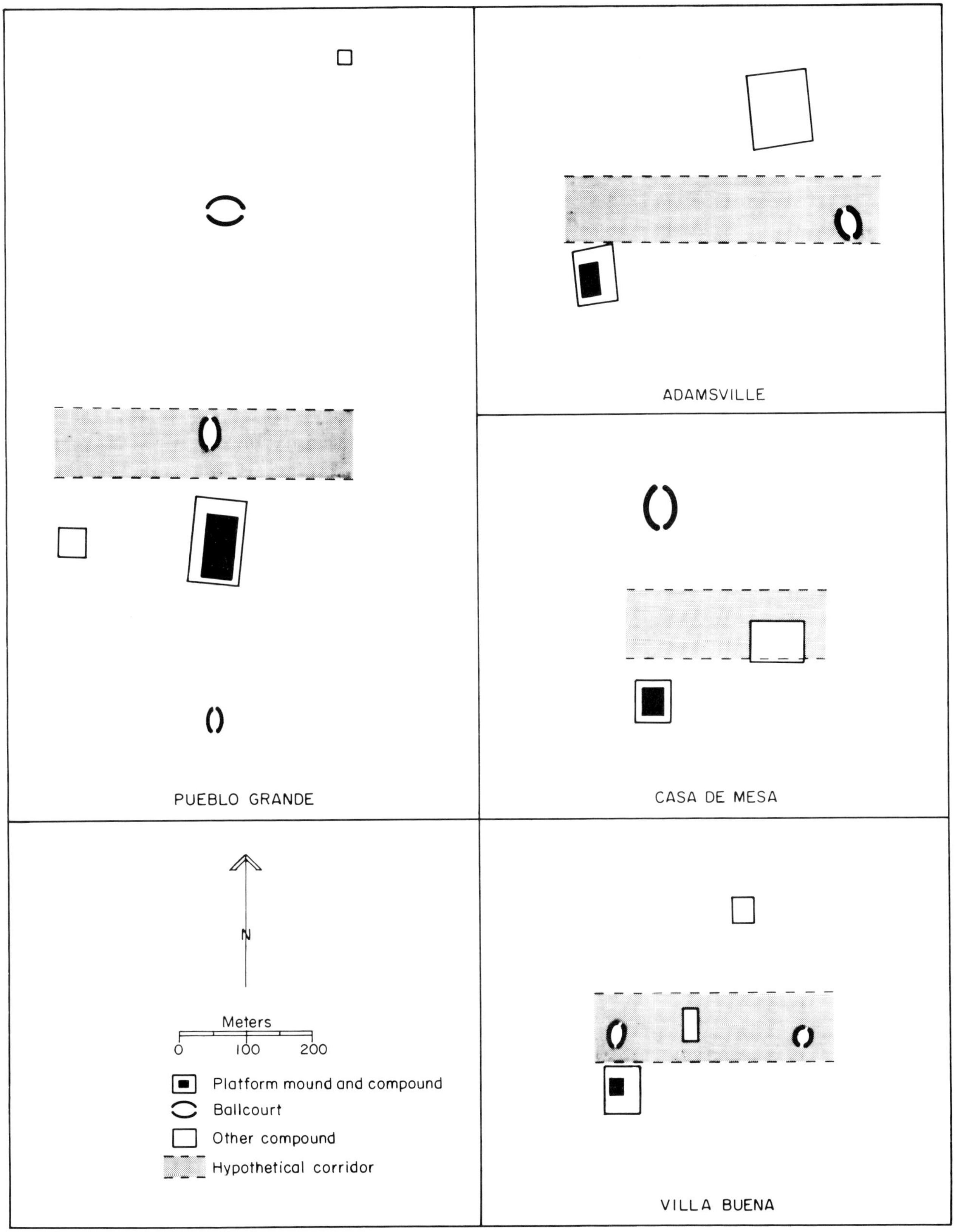

Figure 1.11. The locations of hypothetical corridors relative to platform mounds, compounds, and ballcourts at Casa de Mesa, Adamsville, Pueblo Grande, and Villa Buena.

phase. A Santa Cruz phase occupation may be represented by material in the area of Mound 8 and to the east of that feature in Corridor Area 1.

The freeway corridor represents a linear, east-west transect through the former site area, passing immediately north of the large platform mound designated Mound 7. The corridor contains Mound 8, the smallest of the four platform mounds known to have existed at the site, and the reported location of a ballcourt. Mound 8 was the focus of extensive excavations in 1968, but several features remain partially unexcavated below and immediately adjacent to the mound; it is probable that other features are located in the unexcavated areas to the south, west, and north of the mound. A few small portions of the mound remain unexcavated. The distribution of subsurface features and deposits within the corridor is probably more or less continuous from the eastern margin of Mound 8 to the western portion of Area 5. Because most of Area 6 was unavailable for testing, the distribution of subsurface features and deposits in that area remains essentially unknown; however, the existing evidence suggests that the overall density will be low, except perhaps in the eastern end of the area, nearest Corridor Area 5. Overall feature density in Corridor Area 2 is low, but the remains of a ballcourt may be located in this area. In Area 1, a concentration of features and deposits was revealed by the testing program, primarily clustered in the western portion of that area, and apparently representing a Preclassic occupation. In addition, three canal segments were recorded in Area 1, one of which probably represents a portion of the large Canal Number 5, or Canal Colinas (Turney 1929).

Excavation of a portion of Las Colinas will provide a sample from a type of site which, though extremely important to an understanding of Hohokam prehistory, has received relatively little attention. The identity of the site as a major Classic period locale, as well as the long sequence of occupation present at the site, makes it suitable for the investigation of a variety of research problems. With this general information and these perspectives in mind, we may now turn to the research proposed for the site.

Chapter 2

SITE-SPECIFIC PROBLEM DOMAINS, RESEARCH QUESTIONS, AND DATA REQUIREMENTS

The following section outlines the principal research concerns that will guide the data recovery to be carried out at Las Colinas. Five major problem domains are defined, including: (1) *site structure, growth, and change through time*, (2) *the architectural development and sociopolitical implications of Hohokam platform mounds*, (3) *the nature of the Sedentary-Classic period transition*, (4) *the place of Las Colinas in the Hohokam regional system*, and (5) *process and change in the Hohokam Classic period*. Under each of these general problem domains the significance of the problem and its relevance to current research is discussed, a set of specific research questions is posed, and the general data requirements for each problem domain are considered.

Separate research problems will guide the proposed studies of prehistoric environment and subsistence. While these problems are fundamentally related to the site-specific problems discussed in this chapter, they require a larger, broad-scale data set, and will be presented separately in Chapter 3.

Problem Domain I: Site Structure, Growth, and Change through Time

The project research will focus on a set of interrelated questions dealing with site structure—the basic patterns of organization imposed by a population on the form of their settlement—and the growth of and change in that structure through time. Site structure and related phenomena have recently received important emphasis in Hohokam studies. This emphasis has already produced significant results in terms of our understanding of the overall structure of Hohokam communities, the functional differentiation of space within communities, the size and composition of the social groups that occupied and produced the sites, and the way these patterns of relationships changed through time (Doyel 1974; Wilcox and others 1981; Howard 1982; Gregory 1982, 1984; Sires 1984). As noted above, Classic period platform mound sites exhibit considerable regularity in the arrangement of at least the major architectural features (Gregory 1982). Less is known, however, about the internal structure of these sites on a smaller scale or about the nature of the processes of growth and change that preceded and eventually produced the Classic period settlements (Howard 1982). Excavations at Las Colinas provide an excellent opportunity to examine these problems closely and thus augment and considerably refine the basic data on both the internal structure of Classic period sites and the way that structure emerged from earlier forms. Insight may thereby be gained into the processes that affected the development and transformation of Hohokam society.

Research Questions and Data Requirements

The first task in the study of site structure is to discover and document the temporal and spatial ordering of the cultural features at the site. Once this is accomplished, these data form the basis on which a wide variety of inferences dealing with the functional differentiation of space within the site, the size and composition of the social groups that occupied it, changes in population size and distribution, as well as other concerns, may be generated and tested. Although much of the area within the corridor has been plowed, and although there have been other recent disturbances, the testing program proved that numerous cultural features remain sufficiently intact to be useful in studies of site structure. Extensive horizontal exposures will be required to document the patterns of spatial relationships among the features. Careful study of the depositional processes responsible for producing and filling these features is also required. In addition to the basic excavation data, analysis of artifact associations, chronometric dating techniques, analysis of ceramic assemblages, and detailed examinations of stratigraphic relationships will be employed to resolve temporal issues. Special attention will be paid to the context of all chronometric specimens so that errors of association are not introduced into the interpretations of the dates.

Once the time-space matrix is constructed, the second task is the formulation and testing of hypotheses about changing site structure, as shown on the maps of the feature distributions.

The basic strategy will be to overlay one set of maps over another to search for patterns and relationships. Differential distributions of artifact classes, or of data derived from those classes, can also be displayed on maps and added to the series of overlays. The general goal of this procedure is the construction of a history of the functional differentiation of space and, subsequently, the exploration of the behavioral implications of that history.

In sum, a concern with site structure will provide a broad orientation for the collection and sorting of the basic archaeological data to be recovered from the site, and will provide a basis for addressing the specific issues with particular problem domains.

The following specific research questions will be addressed:

1. *What is the spatial distribution of features and deposits within the corridor area?* Data required to address this question will be obtained from basic excavation procedures. The project will attempt to locate and document all features and deposits within the corridor, and will define horizontal and vertical relationships between features and deposits through mapping and profiling.

2. *What is the temporal distribution of features and deposits within the corridor area?* Again, basic excavation and analysis data are called for. Pottery collections from all proveniences will be sorted into standard types. Where the sample allows, finer seriations of those types may also be attempted. Archaeomagnetic and radiocarbon samples will be collected from appropriate contexts and will serve to verify or refine ceramic sequences. Stratigraphic relationships will be defined and exploited where possible.

3. *How does the spatial and temporal distribution of features and deposits within the corridor relate to what is known of the former extent of the site as a whole?* Once the distribution of features within the corridor is known, the information can be compared to published data on the site as a whole (Gregory and McGuire 1982). Additional information may be obtained by interviewing local residents and by viewing their photographs and collections. One specific approach to be used in manipulating such data is to plot the distribution of known features or deposits on a general site map. Subsequently, the corridor sample can be compared to what is known of the remainder of the site.

4. *What may be inferred concerning the number and variety of features and deposits that may have been destroyed by plowing and other modern activities?* Several lines of evidence will be used. The vertical relationships of features and deposits can be established over the entire corridor, and the effects of plowing and other disturbance can be documented.

   In addition, prehistoric topography can be reconstructed by plotting the depth of the sterile substrate and caliche deposits over the corridor. Such geological evidence can be supplemented by comparing present topography with that on early contour maps of the area, and by seeking documentary data on those historic disturbance factors noted in the field.

5. *How are the functional classes of features (for example pit houses, hornos, cremations, and trash pits) distributed relative to one another; are there overall, atemporal patterns in these distributions (such as an area that was always a plaza), and is there change in their relative distributions over time?* Once features have been classified, they will be sorted by age (at least at the phase level, and possibly into finer divisions based on archaeomagnetic dates, pottery seriations, or stratigraphy). Features of the same age will then be plotted on separate maps; from these, the horizontal relationships between functional classes of features and deposits (as well as changes through time) can be documented. Examples of procedures used in such basic spatial analysis can be found in Wilcox, McGuire, and Sternberg (1981), Gregory (1984), and Howard (1982).

6. *Can the domains of various social groups be identified, and if so, how do they compare with one another and vary through time?* Identification of social units requires the definition of spatially discrete clusters of features within any moment of time. Fortunately, such information will be obtained early in the analysis from the phase maps prepared in response to Question 5. The most promising approach will be to define house clusters or groups which may share outdoor work areas (Wilcox and others 1981; Howard 1982; Gregory 1984). Once the house clusters have been isolated, contemporaneous clusters can be compared in terms of floor space, outdoor activity areas, and so on. Similar comparisons can be made over time, to show changes in the spatial organization of social groups.

7. *Is there evidence for social differentiation among the groups that occupied the site, and did this vary in space of time? How did the social groups vary in size, in activities of production and consumption, in relative access to material goods or other resources, and so forth?* Using the social units defined under Question 5, project members will prepare time-ordered plots of artifacts and biological remains, as well as measures of floor space and other architectural data. Differences in the size and numbers of features will provide the basic means of inferring differences in the size of social units. Architectural variation may also be a useful indicator of social differences. Uneven distributions of shell, painted pottery, intrusive pottery, and other materials may indicate the relative importance of social groups within the site, or over time.

   Social differences may be evident in the production of goods as well as in their consumption. It is therefore important to compare the distribution of production activities as reflected in pollen, faunal, and macrofloral data, as well as by functionally identifiable features such as hornos. Occupational specialization, or differential access to certain basic resources, may be indicated by an analysis of biotic remains, food processing features, and functionally related artifacts.

8. *What influence did the construction of Mounds 7 and 8 have on the use of space around and along trajectories away from these features? Was the zone between Mounds 7 and 8 always a centrally important part of the site or is there evidence at Las Colinas (as there is at other Hohokam sites) that the overall structure of the site was reorganized at the onset of the Classic period*? Answering this question will again rely heavily on the feature distribution maps prepared in response to Question 5. In particular, the Preclassic and Classic period feature distributions must be contrasted. In addition, the Mound 8 construction sequence must be reexamined in order to determine when the mound appeared and began to influence settlement patterns.

9. *If the location of the ballcourt may be determined, what influence did it have on the use of space around it*? If the ballcourt can be located in Area 2 (either in one of the 1968 trench profiles or by cutting new trenches), excavation of the court and surrounding features is called for. The ballcourt and other features can then be incorporated into the phase maps for the corridor, and the distribution of features before and after ballcourt construction can be compared.

10. *How do spatial and temporal distributions of features and deposits at Las Colinas compare to those documented at other sites*? Once the intrasite distribution of features is fully analyzed, it will be possible to compare the Las Colinas site structure with that documented at other sites (such as La Cuidad, Pueblo Grande, and Los Muertos). Published and unpublished data will be used, and the selection of sites for comparison will depend on the nature of the sample recovered from Las Colinas.

Problem Domain II: The Architectural Development and Sociopolitical Implications of Hohokam Platform Mounds

An important emphasis of the research will be on Mound 8 and on the contributions that the further investigation and analysis of the mound and adjacent areas may make to an understanding of the architectural development and sociopolitical implications of Hohokam platform mounds. These two aspects of this problem focus are considered separately below.

The Architectural Development of Hohokam Platform Mounds

With a few minor exceptions, little attention has been paid to the developmental sequence of platform mounds as architectural features (Doyel 1974; Schroeder 1953). This is due at least in part to the fact that only a few of these features have been excavated and well documented (Haury 1976; Wasley 1960; Doyel 1974). As noted above, the known Classic period mounds share a consistent form in that all of them include a massive, rectangular, coursed-caliche retaining wall, which may have internal cells, and which was filled with trash, sterile soil, or some combination of these materials.

Mound 8, too, has a massive coursed-caliche retaining wall, but is unusual in that there are earlier mound units within the massive wall. These earlier units were constructed with post-reinforced caliche retaining walls; one was square in plan, the other rectangular with rounded corners. In this respect, the earlier constructions of Mound 8 have much more in common with the Sedentary period platform mound documented at the Gatlin Site (Wasley 1960) than with the later Classic period forms.

The Gatlin Mound

Wasley's discussion of the Gatlin mound indicates that the exact form of the earliest mound construction is unclear, but it seems to have begun as a small, low feature, possibly similar to Mound 16 at Snaketown (Wasley 1960; Haury 1976; Gregory 1982). The data concerning the later additions are more complete, showing that the mound was enlarged or refurnished at least six times, with the first well-defined structure being in the form of a rough square with rounded corners measuring approximately 10 m by 10 m at the base and 1.5 m in height. Associated with this construction were features that Wasley interpreted as ancillary mounds; he suggests that these smaller units were connected to the main construction by post-reinforced walls (1960, Fig. 5). Subsequent modifications ultimately resulted in a feature that covered the ancillary mounds and was rectangular with rounded corners. This final stage measured approximately 22 m by 27 m at its base and roughly 3 m in height.

Recent reanalysis and reinterpretation of the Gatlin data call into question the existence of at least two of the ancillary mounds, and suggest that the walls of these ancillary features were actually coterminous with the walls of enlargements of the main mound. In addition, the original maps of the site show many more postholes than are present on the maps in the report. The addition of these postholes to the maps and a reexamination of the profiles of the mound suggest that a surrounding palisade may have been a feature of at least five of the mound constructions, and that the palisade of each preceding mound apparently served as a retaining wall for the fill of each subsequent enlargement. Figure 2.1 shows in very basic outline the sequence of mounds and possibly associated palisades that has been derived from our reanalysis of these data. A composite drawing shows the relationships between those stages, providing a perspective on the changes which occurred in size and shape of the mound. The earliest well-defined mound (Stage II) employed a large caliche retaining wall (post reinforced?) which defined the shape of the mound and was filled with mixed trash and soil. This stage of the mound was then topped with a series of successive floors which were placed inside and slightly below the top of the caliche retaining wall. Although this form of construction was used for only one of the mounds in the series, it demonstrates knowledge of a type of construction involving a caliche retaining wall with fill during the Sedentary period.

Mound 8 at Las Colinas

The earliest well-documented mound constructions undertaken at Mound 8 at Las Colinas produced features similar in size and shape to those discovered at Gatlin. The major difference in construction technique is that the early constructions at Mound 8 made much more extensive use of post-reinforced caliche retaining walls than was the case at Gatlin. The construction stages discussed below are illustrated in figure 1.7.

Although Hammack (1981) argues that the construction unit designated "C" on Figure 1.7 was the first to be capped, there is evidence that one or both of the units designated "A" and "B" once stood alone as mounds and were probably capped in some fashion. A floor was present in the fill of at least two of the cells associated with Unit A, and an alignment of postholes was present in this floor (Hammack 1981). Although Hammack suggests that these were loom holes, this seems implausible. They compare favorably, however, to the alignment of postholes discovered on top of the Gatlin mound, Stage III (Wasley 1960, Fig. 10). Note that the post-reinforced walls within Units A and B form cells of various shapes and sizes. Note also that Unit A may have had a surrounding palisade similar to those described for Mound 16 at Snaketown (Haury 1976) and for the several stages of the Gatlin mound.

The ceramic materials recovered from the fill of the early Mound 8 constructions, as well as archaeomagnetic dates obtained from stratigraphically associated features, indicate that Units A, B, and C were erected during the Soho phase of the Classic period. Thus mounds quite similar in size and shape to the Sedentary period forms at Gatlin continued to be built into the early part of the Classic period, with minor modifications in construction techniques.

Additional similarities between the Gatlin Mound and Mound 8 could be noted. For the present, it is sufficient to point out that Mound 8 may represent a bridge between the techniques of platform mound construction in use during the Sedentary period and those which came to be common during the Soho phase of the Classic period. If the palisades prove to be consistent features of Sedentary and early Classic period construction, then it may be that they are precursors of the rectangular compound walls which are subsequently a consistent companion to platform mounds. As noted above, Mound 8 is the only known Classic period platform mound without a surrounding compound wall. Determining whether or not such a feature once existed is important in documenting the relationship between Mound 8 and other Classic period mounds, and may shed further light on the hypothesis that palisades and compound walls are developmentally related.

The Function and Sociopolitical Implications of Hohokam Platform Mounds

Logically related to questions about the architectural development of platform mounds are questions about the functions of these features and how those functions may have changed through time. Clearly, the functions of these features were related to the activities of groups of people within the society who determined that the mounds should be built as well as how they should be built, and who were somehow able to organize and direct their construction. The existing data suggest that the Sedentary period and probably early Soho phase forms did not themselves serve as the loci of residential units, because they lacked houses. They probably were instead the focus of some specialized, perhaps ritual, activity. It appears that an important shift in the overall function of these features occurred during the early part of the Classic period, and that they were subsequently used as residential space by some segment of the population. While most of the features on the top of Mound 8 had been largely destroyed prior to the 1968 excavations, the recording of remnants of several structures on top of the mound indicates that Mound 8 did indeed serve as residential space during the Soho phase.

Research Questions and Data Requirements

The data collected from the Mound 8 area in 1968 remain largely uninterpreted with respect to the problems of mound function and the nature of the social groups associated with the mound. The proposed research provides an opportunity to augment the empirical data as well as to undertake a detailed study and interpretation of the changing structure of space around the mound, based on the data collected in 1968. This will lead to inferences concerning the function of the mound and the nature of the social groups most closely associated with the mound. Because the features that formerly stood on top of the mound are not available for study, the examination of the function of the mound and of related questions concerning the nature of the social groups associated with the

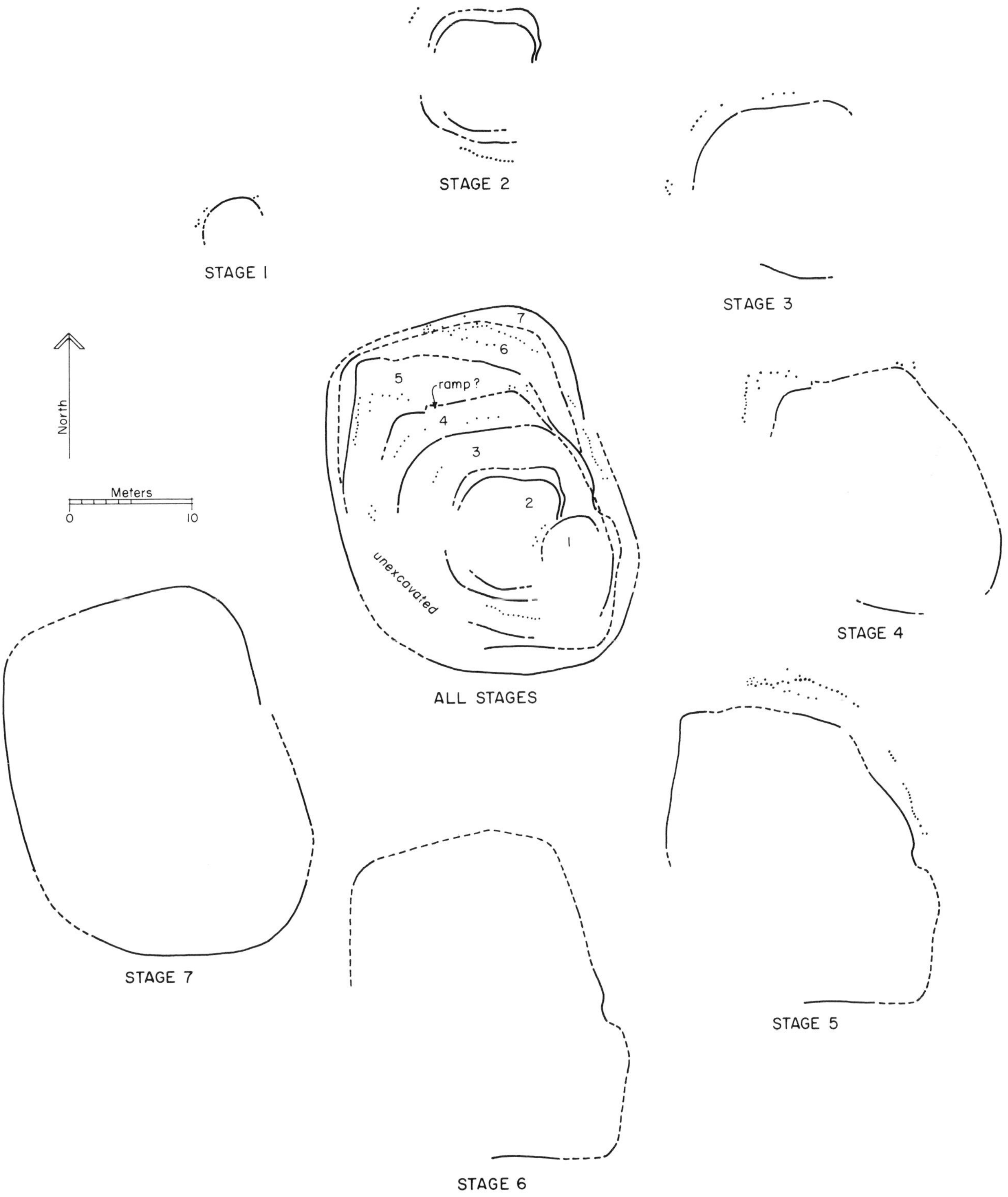

Figure 2.1. Construction sequence at the Gatlin mound, Stages I through VII (after Wasley 1960).

mound must be accomplished by reconstructing the sequential use of space in the immediate area of the mound, by contrasting the characteristics of that use of space with areas away from the mound, and by the compilation of comparative data from other sites. Specifically, we wish to know what kinds of activities were carried out in the area immediately surrounding the mound and how those activities may have changed during the period of occupation. If the mound and the area surrounding it were in fact the residential space occupied by groups of high social status, then we would expect differences in architecture and in the artifact assemblages between this area and contemporaneous features and deposits away from the mound.

Several additional classes of data will be required to deal with this aspect of the research, and focusing on this set of problems dictates that several different strategies be followed. First, it will be necessary to reexamine and reinterpret the construction sequence of Mound 8. Although much of the mound fill was removed during the excavations and some of the walls were subsequently knocked down as a safety measure, there are several small areas of the mound which were not completely excavated, as well as places where profiles may be cut through the remaining deposits (Hammack and Sullivan 1981, Map 1). In particular, the question of which construction units stood alone, and the presence or absence of palisades associated with various construction stages can be addressed. Further, it is important to determine whether or not an earlier mound construction existed. Such a structure may be represented by the massive truncated wall in the center of Mound 8, and possibly by the long, post-reinforced wall that extends beneath and to the south of the series of mound constructions. It will be necessary to excavate the remaining features and deposits to the east and south of the mound, as well as the remaining portions of the features under and adjacent to it which were not completely excavated during the 1968 work. The existence of a compound wall surrounding Mound 8 will also be examined, and, if one is present, its size, extent, and age will be determined, if possible.

In sum, our overall strategy is to reconstruct the sequential use of space in and around the mound area and to relate the use of that space to the reinterpreted sequence of mound construction. Toward that end, the following research questions dealing with the architectural development, functions, and sociopolitical implications of platform mounds will be addressed.

1. *Which of the construction units within Mound 8 stood as separate platforms?*

2. *Was there a palisade around any of the Mound 8 constructions?*

3. *What additional evidence exists for a mound construction in the area of Mound 8 that predates those documented by Hammack?*

4. *Was there a compound wall around Mound 8; to what stage or stages of mound construction does it relate?*

   Information from the 1968 excavations (Hammack and Sullivan 1981) will be combined with new data to be collected in order to address these four questions. The primary approach will necessarily be architectural and stratigraphic, documenting the sequence of additions and superpositions in plans and profiles. In particular, the 1968 profiles must be reassessed and supplementary profiles must be cut. Ceramic, archaeomagnetic, and, if needed, radiocarbon dates will be obtained for features and deposits within the mound in order to verify the architectural and stratigraphic reconstruction. Such dating techniques will also permit the assignment of absolute dates to the various construction units.

5. *How do the houses and other features around Mound 8 relate to the various stages of mound construction?* Once the construction of the mound, palisades, and compound wall is documented, it will be necessary to relate these units to houses and other features in their vicinity. When such features are excavated, it will be especially important to document their stratigraphic relationships to the various phases of mound construction as well as their age relative to one another. This implies a concern with fine stratigraphic distinctions; in order to obtain the level of stratigraphic control needed, both conventional recording techniques and thermal-infrared photography will be used.

   Ceramic and chronometric dating of samples will verify such microstratigraphy where it exists, and will provide dates where stratigraphic relationships cannot be defined.

6. *What may be inferred about the nature of the social groups that occupied Mound 8 and the immediately surrounding area; what changes in these groups occurred through time?* The procedures used elsewhere on the site for identifying contemporaneous house groups, social differentiation, and change through time will be extended to the Mound 8 precinct. As social units are defined and compared, it will be important to assess the distortions caused by "missing" data for the area on top of the mound.

7. *What activities were carried out in the area surrounding Mound 8, and how do these compare with the activities carried out in other parts of the site?* The maps prepared for Problem Domain I, Question 5, showing the temporal and spatial distributions of functional classes, can also be used here. Features in the mound area defined as living space, work areas and such (based on form, size, and artifactual and biotic content) can be contrasted with features found elsewhere in the site. If possible, changes in the degree of functional differentiation between mound and nonmound areas will be documented.

8. *How does the range of artifact classes recovered from Mound 8 compare with that documented for other portions of the site?*

9. *How does the changing structure of space around Mound 8 compare with that documented around platform mounds at other sites (for example Escalante, Mesa Grande, Los Hornos, and Los Muertos)?*

Problem Domain III: The Nature of the Sedentary-Classic Period Transition

The likelihood that a substantial number of Sedentary period features and deposits will be recorded within the corridor area, in combination with the already documented Soho phase (Classic period) occupation of the site, makes Las Colinas an appropriate context in which to examine a set of research problems dealing with the Sedentary-Classic period transition. These problems define another major focus of project research.

The earliest studies of Hohokam archaeology noted that major changes occurred within that society toward the end of the Sedentary period (or A.D. 1100, as the period is now dated). Long-standing interpretations have focused on differences in architecture and other aspects of material culture between the two periods, and have held that these changes were due in large part to the presence of new ethnic populations in the Hohokam area. These groups have been most often referred to as Salado (Gumerman and Haury 1979; Doyel and Haury 1976). More recently, these interpretations have been challenged as an increasing body of data has provided evidence that changes in material culture were not as drastic as previously thought. For example, research on the Salt-Gila Aqueduct Project has demonstrated continuity in ceramic technology and architectural forms for the transition (Abbott 1982; Sires 1982). Well-defined Hohokam patterns may thus be shown to continue into the Classic period. This perspective is also suggested above in relation to the development of Hohokam platform mounds.

Nonetheless, significant changes did occur. A drastic reduction in the scale of the Hohokam regional system is indicated at the end of the Sedentary period. During the Sedentary, as evidenced by ballcourt distributions (Wilcox and Sternberg 1983), the Phoenix Basin was the center of an extensive system of interaction that extended to Gila Bend on the west, to Flagstaff on the north, to the Tucson Basin on the south, and to the Animas Valley on the east. At the end of the Sedentary period, sites in Gila Bend, the lower Verde Valley, and the Buttes Dam area were abandoned, as was Snaketown in the Phoenix Basin. Most sites in the Phoenix Basin persisted, though many were reorganized, and parts of the Queen Creek area were abandoned (Teague 1982). The Salt River Valley appears to have witnessed a population increase relative to the middle Gila, while in both areas the canal systems may have been consolidated into larger systems (Wilcox 1979; Masse 1981; Nicholas 1983). Exchange connections with populations outside the Phoenix Basin during the Soho phase seem to have been limited, suggesting that the remaining system was more isolated and circumscribed than at any earlier time (Doyel 1980). It is in this context that a new form of organization, expressed by the Soho phase forms of the platform mounds and their distribution, came into being; shortly afterward, renewed outside contacts are indicated (Doyel 1980).

A variety of characterizations and explanations of these changes have been suggested. These include, among others, the cessation of Mesoamerican contacts (Haury 1976), population growth or pressure (Grady 1976), environmental instability (Weaver 1972; Grebinger 1971; Plog 1980), or some combination of these (compare Doyel 1980; Teague 1982).

Doyel (1980) has defined three research topics bearing on the problem of the Sedentary-Classic period transition: (1) the nature of the natural environment and the subsistence strategies employed by the Hohokam; (2) the character and degree of social differentiation that was present before and that may have developed during and after the transition; and (3) the magnitude and distribution of population. To these we may add: (4) the nature of trade and exchange, and (5) the ethnic composition of Classic period society.

Environment and Subsistence

Many researchers have assessed the Sedentary to Classic period transition in light of postulated environmental changes. It is thus important to collect and assess environmental data from features and deposits spanning this time period. It has been suggested that the transition was accompanied by a consolidation of the existing canal systems (Haury 1976; Wilcox 1979; Masse 1981). Given the presence of several canal segments in the corridor, an attempt will be made to date these features and to evaluate their relationship with contemporaneous architectural features. Through studies of environmental and subsistence data, it should also be possible to assess the impact such a postulated change in agricultural technology might have had on the subsistence base.

Social Organization and Differentiation

Doyel has suggested that the social organization of the Preclassic and Classic period populations should be examined more closely (1980). It will be possible to do this at Las Colinas through several means. First, it will be necessary to examine the platform mound and the area surrounding the mound in greater detail. The architectural development of the platform mounds proposed above is significant in that it suggests that their development spanned the Sedentary-Classic transition in orderly fashion. If it can be shown that the above reinterpretation of Mound 8 is essentially correct and that there was an even earlier mound feature present in the area of Mound 8, this would be critical to an understanding of the character of changes which occurred during this time period. Second, the possible presence of another important architectural feature—the ballcourt—is of considerable significance for an understanding of the Sedentary period identity of the site. Wilcox (Wilcox and Sternberg 1983) has shown that the distribution of ballcourts retracts at the end of the Sedentary period. If a ballcourt is identified, it may then be possible to determine when it was constructed and how long it was used, thus clarifying its place in the site's changing structure. In general, we wish to determine whether there is evidence for changes in the kind and degree of social differentiation between the Sedentary and Classic periods at the site.

Population

In order to assess the impact of changes in population during the transition, an attempt must be made to estimate the relative population sizes. In the absence of a reliable sample of materials from the Salt and Gila valleys, this has been impossible to do; however, given the continuity of occupation at Las Colinas, it will be possible to examine the population size for this portion of the larger site area, and to ascertain how this population developed through time, using the kinds of site structure data gathered in relation to the first general problem domain above. Doyel's hypothesis of no population growth during the transition may thus be tested here against Wilcox' contention that there was local growth in the Salt River Valley (1979; see also Upham and Rice 1980).

Trade and Exchange

It is clear from previous studies that the Sedentary-Classic transition witnessed a shift in the focus of Hohokam trade and exchange. Changes in materials available to the groups living at Las Colinas can be documented for the transition and the origins of the materials ascertained in an attempt to understand the direction of, and the causes behind, this shift.

Ethnic Composition

The hypothesized Salado or Puebloan intrusion into the Hohokam area during the Sedentary-Classic period transition has been challenged, but has not been entirely put to rest (Haury 1976). The data available at present, in particular those from the Salt-Gila Aqueduct Project, tend to refute many of the assumptions about the general nature of Preclassic and Classic period Hohokam society upon which this interpretation has been based (Teague 1982). Nonetheless, while existing arguments for this reconstruction may have been severely damaged, final resolution of this question requires examination of changes during the period at a major center. To date, there have been no such thorough excavations of a central site spanning the transition and the full Classic period. Las Colinas provides an opportunity to address this problem in a context in which evidence of intrusive populations in a position of cultural dominance should be most readily apparent, if it exists at all.

Research Questions and Data Requirements

The data recovered from excavations at Las Colinas should be highly appropriate to address these issues. The nature of the site during the Classic period is already quite apparent and it should be possible to enlarge that picture further, elaborating on the sequence of changes during the Soho phase. The existence of numerous Sacaton phase features is likely, and it should be possible to clarify questions about the size and relative importance of the site prior to the Classic period. The discovery, excavation, and dating of the ballcourt will be particularly important in this regard, as the presence or absence of a ballcourt at the site during the Sedentary period is significant in assessing the role of the site during this period (Wilcox and Sternberg 1983). The possibility that the remains of a Sedentary period platform mound exist is also important. This question will be addressed by the planned excavations in the area of Mound 8 and by the reanalysis and reinterpretation of that feature.

These research topics may be structured as a series of comparisons between the Sedentary period and Classic period Soho phase remains to be documented at Las Colinas, and by examination of those materials (if any) which actually fall within the transition period (A.D. 1050 to A.D. 1150). The following research questions will be addressed.

1. *Were there differences in the size and composition of contemporaneous social groups that occupied the site? What changes occur in the size and composition of social groups between the Sedentary and Classic periods?*
2. *Is there evidence of the differential distribution of shell and other materials of nonlocal origin?*
3. *Is there evidence of the differential distribution of foodstuffs?*
4. *Is there evidence of specialization in the production of either foodstuffs or material goods?*
5. *What changes occur in the structure of the site between the Sedentary and Classic periods? What do these changes imply about the nature of social differentiation?*

   These questions relating to the Sedentary-Classic transition may be seen as more specific reiterations of earlier research questions. They will be addressed using relevant portions of the data amassed in relation to Questions 5 through 9 of Problem Domain I and Questions 5 through 8 of Problem Domain II, this time focusing specifically on the changes taking place during the Sacaton-Soho phase transition.

6. *What may be inferred about the prehistoric environment during the Sedentary-Classic transition with respect to temperature, effective moisture, and other variables that might have affected the effectiveness and relative productivity of Hohokam subsistence strategies*? A variety of approaches will be used to answer this question. Biological samples (pollen, flotation, and charcoal and bone from screening) will be submitted for species identification. The materials will also be ordered chronologically, so that the changing frequencies of economic and noneconomic species can be shown; some of these changes will no doubt prove to reflect environmental shifts.

   Additional information on the prehistoric setting will be obtained by examination of tree-ring data from the Salt and Gila drainages. With historic streamflow and tree-ring data as a base, the project will use archaeological tree-ring values to reconstruct Salt River streamflow and Palmer Drought Severity indexes for the period of Hohokam occupation.

   It should also be possible to obtain environmental data from the samples to be taken from canal profiles. Effective use of such data will depend on the project's ability to date the canal sediments.

7. *What evidence exists for changes in subsistence practices and, in particular, for changes in the character of the major canal systems that may have served the site*? Changes in subsistence practices will be inferred in part from pollen, faunal, and macrofloral samples, as ordered chronologically by ceramic and other dating means. This approach will be supplemented by a study of the temporal distributions of artifacts and features that are thought to be used in particular food-processing tasks. Specific field strategies for the canal study are provided in Chapter 5. The data from that study, along with published and unpublished information, should allow the project to document changes in the canal networks serving the site.

8. *Are there patterned differences in burial practices that may be related to social differentiation*? *Are there differences in the artifacts associated with burials (cremations and inhumations) that may indicate differences in social status*? Human remains will be submitted for physical anthropological study, and the date and mode of burial, as well as associated features and remains, will be documented. From these data it should be possible to document any patterned differences in burial practices, as well as the presence or absence of change from the Sacaton to Soho phase.

9. *What may be inferred about the relative differences in the population of the site between the Sedentary and Classic periods*? Once habitation structures are identified and dated, it will be necessary to estimate the number of contemporaneous houses during each phase of the Sedentary and Classic periods. Because of disturbance (along with other factors) minimum and maximum estimates will be necessary.

   Once the houses have been ordered in time, total floor areas will be calculated; the resulting figures will be used to create population estimates. Differences from one phase to the next can then be noted.

10. *What changes occur in the number and variety of nonlocal items reaching the site*? Within the Sacaton and Soho phase assemblages, nonlocal material will be identified and their functional contexts noted. Changing frequencies of given materials or items will be noted and explanations for any such changes will be sought. (Some of the data needed to answer this question also apply to Question 7 of Problem Domain I).

11. *What changes occur in the ultimate sources of nonlocal items reaching the site*? This question will focus on the same items as Question 10. For pottery, ultimate sources can be estiablished typologically, while the origins of shell and certain other biological remains can be established by reference to known species distributions. For other materials, specialized analyses of carefully selected samples may be necessary (for example, trace element analysis of obsidian).

12. *What evidence exists for a change in the ethnic composition of the site between the Sedentary and Classic periods*? *If such a change is shown to exist, what is its character and magnitude*? This question will be difficult (if not impossible) to resolve, but it must be addressed in view of the hypothesized "Salado intrusion" at the onset of the Soho phase; archaeological and osteological data will be used. The traditional hallmarks of the immigrant Salado—new burial practices, architectural forms, and ceramic and other artifact types—should certainly diverge from earlier forms at the site if such a migrant group arrived during the Soho phase. Depending on the size and character of the burial population recovered, it may be possible to determine whether or not different genetic populations are present in the sample. Differences in burial goods may also indicate ethnic diversity (Schreiber and others 1981).

Problem Domain IV: The Place of Las Colinas in the Classic Period Hohokam Regional System

Recent directions taken in Hohokam archaeological studies emphasize a regional perspective, viewing the Hohokam phenomenon as a regional system (Wilcox 1979). This perspective suggests that an important question to be addressed is the place that Las Colinas occupied in that system, especially during the Classic period.

In order to understand the position of Las Colinas in the Classic period Hohokam regional system, it is necessary to review what is known of the distribution and locational characteristics of Classic period sites with platform mounds. As discussed earlier, at least 38 such sites were once distributed throughout the Phoenix Basin. Figure 1.1 shows the overall distribution of Classic period sites with platform mounds, and indicates that the distribution of these sites is more dense in the Salt drainage than in the Gila. This distribution parallels that of canals in the respective areas; of the 38 known sites with platform mounds, only 2 are not located on major canal systems. Furthermore, in most cases more than one platform mound site is located on the same canal system. For example, on the large Casa Grande Canal there are five such sites including Casa Grande, which is located at the end of the canal (Midvale 1965). In those cases where more than one platform mound site is located on the same canal system, their spacing is quite regular. For example, La Ciudad is approximately three miles east of Las Colinas, and approximately three miles west of Pueblo Grande. Plaza Tempe was located near the head of the long canal on the south side of the Salt River, on which Pueblo del Monte, Las Canopas, and Pueblo Viejo were situated. All of these sites have platform mounds and are located at intervals of three miles from one another along this canal.

It has been suggested that the canal systems were consolidated during the Classic period (Haury 1976; Wilcox 1979; Nicholas 1983) and it is probably not coincidental that the very regular and closely spaced distribution of platform mounds occurs at this time. This suggests that political units above the level of the site were somehow functionally related to the major canal systems, and that Doyel's concept of an irrigation community must be reexamined and modified (1980). A highly organized system of control and communication may have been necessary for the maintenance of the canal systems.

In order to understand Las Colinas in the context of the regional system, it will be necessary to further examine the complex distribution of platform mound sites along the canal system, the significance of this distribution, and the function of Las Colinas within it. Preliminary considerations suggest that 6 of the 38 platform mound sites may have played a more dominant role in political decision-making than the others. The basis for this hypothesis is the fact that these six sites either have more than one platform mound (Las Colinas and Casa Grande), or have much larger compounds and platform mounds than the others (Fig. 1.3). Las Colinas has the largest compounds, and the most platform mounds, and is laid out on the largest scale of any known Classic period site. Like Casa Grande and Casa Blanca in the Gila River Valley, and like Pueblo Viejo, Mesa Grande, Pueblo Grande, and perhaps Los Muertos in the Salt, Las Colinas may have occupied the highest level in the site hierarchy, in which smaller sites with platform mounds as well as sites without mounds occupied the lower levels. Yet there is no reason to believe that Las Colinas occupied a similar position in the preceding Sedentary period regional system (Wilcox and Sternberg 1983). Therefore, work at Las Colinas affords an opportunity to study what may have been a principal political center in the Classic period, to investigate its relationship to other sites with platform mounds and to the major canal systems, and to explore the reasons it became such an important site. In this way, research at Las Colinas can contribute significantly to a better understanding of the changing structure of the Hohokam regional system as a whole.

Research Questions and Data Requirements

The following research questions dealing with the Classic period Hohokam regional system and the place of Las Colinas in that system will be addressed.

1. *What may be inferred about the nature of the Classic period regional system with respect to the variables of scale, integration, and complexity?*

2. *What is the relationship between the distribution of platform mound sites and the canal systems, especially relative to the labor and organization required to maintain and coordinate use of the canal systems? How does Las Colinas fit into these relationships?*

3. *What evidence exists for a Classic period settlement heirarchy, particularly with respect to the possible differentiation of those sites with platform mounds? What is the place of Las Colinas in that hierarchy?*

4. *How was the development of the Classic period regional system conditioned and structured by the system that existed in the preceding Sedentary period?*

These are broad-scale, orienting questions designed to look forward to the synthesis and interpretation of the data collected from Las Colinas. Their goal is to determine what the Las Colinas materials indicate about the Classic period Hohokam regional system.

Much of the data needed to address these questions consists of published and unpublished information on Classic period sites, some of which has already been analyzed and summarized elsewhere (Gregory 1982). This information will be augmented by and reinterpreted in light of the results of the work at Las Colinas. In particular, the relationship between the distribution of platform mound sites and the canal systems may be elucidated by the studies of the canals at Las Colinas and the larger canal systems in which they functioned.

Problem Domain V: Process and Change in the Hohokam Classic Period

While the Sedentary-to-Classic-period transition has received attention recently (Doyel 1980), less work has been focused on the changes which occurred *during* the Classic period that ultimately resulted in the decline and disappearance of the Hohokam cultural system as it is known prehistorically. This has been due in part to an overall lack of data pertaining to the Soho phase, a circumstance that has only recently begun to be remedied (Sires 1982; Ferg 1984; Abbott 1982). The demonstrable existence of a Classic period sequence at Las Colinas, including early, middle, and late Soho and Civano phase features (Hammack 1981), makes it an excellent context in which to study the important changes within the Classic period. Two aspects of this problem are of particular importance to project research: (1) the dating of the Classic period Soho and Civano phases and the relationship of those phases to the processes that operated during the Classic period, and (2) the disappearance and decline of the Hohokam cultural system.

The Dating of Classic Period Phases

The appearance of well-dated Gila Polychrome pottery in conjunction with purported changes in architecture has served as a marker for the beginning of the Civano phase, now dated between A.D. 1300 and A.D. 1450. It can now be shown, however, that the pattern of architectural changes is not as clear cut as was once thought (Sires 1982; Ferg 1984); it may be that the current division of the Classic period into phases is inappropriate and misleading with respect to the processes that operated during the period. Although the Great House at Casa Grande was built during the Civano phase (Wilcox and Shenk 1977; Wilcox and Sternberg 1981), most platform mounds appear to have been constructed during the Soho phase and used into the Civano (Schroeder 1953; Doyel 1974; Gregory 1982). If the presence of these features marks an overall continuity in the Hohokam system, as the present evidence suggests, then the A.D. 1300 date may prove to be an arbitrary division that implies little about the structure of changing systemic conditions affecting the evolution of Hohokam society. On the other hand, the convenient marker provided by Gila Polychrome may be an indication of significant regional developments in the alliances of Phoenix Basin populations.

A good series of archaeomagnetic dates spanning the Classic period already exists for the features around Mound 8. It may be legitimately expected that this series will be augmented by the proposed data recovery, and that ceramic or relative stratigraphic dating of most structures will be possible with or without suitable chronometric samples. Such a temporal ordering of features, combined with the analysis of site structure suggested above, as well as a time-ordered series of environmental data, should greatly enhance our understanding of the social and environmental processes that operated during the Classic period. This, in turn, will provide a basis for reinterpreting the present chronological division of the classic period.

The Decline and Disappearance of the Hohokam Cultural System

Shortly after the massive, caliche-walled platform mounds were built, probably during the middle to late Soho phase, Gila Polychrome began to appear in quantity in the Phoenix Basin. This pottery type is widespread, occurring in a huge area from the Phoenix and Tucson basins to the Cliff area of New Mexico, to Zuni, and to Casas Grandes in the south (Doyel and Haury 1976). During the Civano phase, the occupants of the Phoenix Basin apparently participated in a larger regional system that may have brought in the Gila Polychrome and probably other materials as well. Data from Las Colinas, however, suggest that the organization of that system probably changed significantly during the Civano phase. Mound 8 no longer served as a special place and the area was apparently converted to ordinary domestic use, only to be abandoned altogether around A.D. 1450.

Five structures recorded during the 1968 excavations near Mound 8 produced archaeomagnetic dates that place their occupation at or near the end of the Civano phase as it is currently defined (Features 34, 35, 40A, 41, 42, and 74). These structures cluster in three areas around the mound, and appear to represent the residences and associated living spaces of small social groups, perhaps on the order of extended families. Although it did not produce an ar chaeomagnetic date, a sixth structure adjacent to Feature 41 (Feature 42) probably also represents this late period of occupation. A small, post-reinforced caliche wall connects this structure in haphazard fashion to the northeast corner of Mound 8. At least two of the structures (Features 41 and 42) appear to have been constructed with no particular attention to the orientation and integrity of Mound 8 itself. Ceramics associated with the latest of these structures (archaeomagetically dated at A.D. 1450 $\pm$ 17) were found to be cruder both stylistically and technologically than earlier Hohokam ceramics, and to have several characteristics suggestive of Piman pottery (Crown 1981a: 107). This evidence suggests that an area that for centuries had been a special precinct was converted to use as ordinary domestic space. A similar sequence of events has been suggested for the Big House at Casa Grande (Wilcox and Sternberg 1981).

Factors advanced to account for the demise of the Hohokam system as it existed during the Soho phase (and for at least part of the Civano phase) include environmental degradation, internecine warfare, disease, and invasion. At present, little solid evidence can be garnered in support of any of these alternatives. One reason for this is the lack of data: very few documented sites were occupied into the terminal Classic period.

The late Civano phase materials from Las Colinas described above suggest that, whatever the explanation of the decline may be, it was accompanied by organizational change(s). If we presume that the same genetic populations that occupied the late structures at Las Colinas were also responsible for the construction, enlargement, and use of Mound 8, then it is clear that these populations did not live the same kind of lives in A.D. 1450 that they had from A.D. 1300 to 1350.

The project therefore offers an opportunity to more fully document these drastic changes and to investigate the processes that produced them. This may be done both by recording any additional Civano phase features that may be present and by relating these, and the features recorded by Hammack (1981), to a more comprehensive picture of changing site structure, both immediately around Mound 8 and farther away from the mound to the east and west.

Research Questions and Data Requirements

Given the foregoing considerations, the following questions may be posed with respect to the dating and character of the Classic period phases, and the study of process and change during the Classic period.

1. *Was the present phase breakdown of the Classic period appropriate with respect to the processes that operated during the period*? To answer this question, basic excavation data from Classic period deposits must be carefully ordered using stratigraphic data and other means of relative dating. Any absolute dates obtained for these deposits will also be important. Once the sequence of deposits is established, the various types of remains must be examined to estalish patterns of continuity or change over time. Stylistic changes in architecture and artifacts can be noted; subsistence changes can be noted through shifts in the relative frequencies of biological remains (see Questions 3 and 4 of Problem Domain III). Ultimately, the utility of the Soho-Civano phase distinction in understanding processes of change at Las Colinas may be evaluated.

2. *What is the significance of the appearance of Gila Polychrome at A.D. 1300; what other changes occurred at this time*? Once patterns of change within the Classic period have been defined, it will be important to identify contexts in which Gila Polychrome occurs. Available archaeomagnetic and radiocarbon dates should be used to bracket the initial appearance of the type at Las Colinas. Correlations between the type's appearance and other changes can then be noted.

3. *Is there a more appropriate way in which to divide the Classic period*? Clearly, the answer to this question depends on the results of the previously defined questions.

4. *Based on the evidence from Las Colinas, what was the nature of the organizational changes that took place during the Civano phase*? This question will require basic information from excavation and analysis of Civano phase remains: stratigraphic, architectural, artifactual, and biological data are all called for. These investigations will parallel those outlined under Problem Domain III, focusing this time on the Civano phase rather than the Sedentary-Classic period transition. Once the nature of the Civano phase occupation at Las Colinas has been defined, it will be interesting to compare these results with data from other sites.

5. *What processes were responsible for these changes that resulted in so radical a transformation in the way places like Mound 8 and the Casa Grande were perceived and used, and how are those processes related to those that soon thereafter led to the abandonment of all remaining Hohokam sites*? This question looks forward to the data synthesis obtained by answering Questions 1 through 4. Depending on the results of the attempts to define organizational changes, changes in the effective environment, subsistence practices, and population, it may be possible to isolate and quantify those factors that were responsible.

6. *Was the collapse of a more complex form of political organization a prelude to regional abandonment*? This question is related to Problem Domain IV (the place of Las Colinas in the Classic period Hohokam regional system), as well as to the five questions presented above. Resolution of the issues involved will require comparative analysis of existing data from a number of Hohokam sites, in light of the results from Las Colinas.

7. *If a nonelite population was still in place in the early 1400s, why did it abandon an area that had been sucessfully inhabited by sedentary farmers for a millennium or more? What became of these people*? As with Question 4, the full range of basic excavation and analysis data will be required from Civano phase deposits. Any post-1400 remains encountered will need to be analyzed in terms of possible social or subsistence stress, especially in comparison to earlier periods. Environmental data from these deposits, as well as the canal and streamflow studies may also be appropriate to understanding the abandonment of the site.

8. *Is there additional evidence at Las Colinas that may link the latest occupation of the site to the early historic Pima who lived on the nearby Gila River*? At Las Colinas,

the key evidence relating to the Hohokam-Pima continuum consists of pottery from late Civano phase contexts (Crown 1981a). Late deposits (from the current field season or recovered in 1968) must be identified, and the characteristics of pottery from such contexts and their similarity to early Pima wares must be evaluated. Analysis of architecture and nonceramic remains should also be carried out in order to provide supplementary information on similarities and differences between late Hohokam and early Pima culture.

Summary

The foregoing sections have presented the basic research orientation which will be followed in the data recovery at Las Colinas. The research emphases proposed reflect the rapidly changing nature of Hohokam research at present, and the special contribution that excavations at Las Colinas may make to this research.

Significant advances in knowledge of the material culture, economy, and social organization of the Hohokam during the period of occupation at Las Colinas are in progress through various studies in central and southern Arizona. One of these, the Salt-Gila Aqueduct Project, has significantly altered the available data concerning changes in the general nature of Hohokam society between the Santa Cruz phase (the earliest known occupation at Las Colinas) and the Civano phase. Further, that project and others addressing similar problems have also focused attention on variability within the Hohokam regional system as an important element in interpretation of stability and change in that system. Such variability has yet to be adequately documented for the central Salt River Valley, an area that is crucial to an understanding of Classic period developments, given evidence of population redistribution and increasing importance of the area as a population center during this period. Major village sites in the core area, where many of the hypothesized Classic period developments should be most evident, have generally lain outside the scope of those studies.

As information from projects like Salt-Gila suggests (Teague 1982), the real changes in Hohokam society during the Classic may be related to changes in subsistence strategies emphasizing: (1) riverine agriculture, (2) redistribution of population into riverine areas and in particular into the Salt River Valley, and (3) subsequent modification and elaboration at the higher levels of social and political intergration. If so, then Las Colinas provides an ideal opportunity for significant advances in our understanding of the Hohokam. Because of the importance of environmentally determined, subsistence-related behavior in these developments, a series of problem domains have been identified to guide research in that area. These will be outlined in Chapter 3.

Chapter 3

STUDIES OF PREHISTORIC ENVIRONMENT AND SUBSISTENCE

Environmental variables have been invoked in various ways as important factors in understanding Hohokam prehistory, particularly with reference to developments during the Classic period (Grady 1976; Weaver 1972; Doyel 1980; Wilcox 1979). The range of environmental data to be collected from Las Colinas will make a substantial contribution to the further understanding of: (1) the nature of the prehistoric environment and changes, natural and man-made, that occurred in various aspects of that environment; (2) the effects of environmental change on the prehistoric populations; and (3) the methods and strategies employed by the prehistoric populations in articulating with the natural and culturally modified environments. These general concerns obviously represent a complex and interrelated set of topics, which may be broken down into the following problem domains: *environmental reconstruction*, *irrigation technology*, and *the Hohokam subsistence base*.

Problem Domain I: Environmental Reconstruction

It has been argued that variation in effective moisture during the period from A.D. 1000 to 1475 played a significant role in the course of Hohokam development. Based on palynological evidence, Weaver (1972) has proposed a sequence of relative changes in effective moisture within the Salt River Valley for this period. He suggests that the periods from A.D. 1000 to 1075 and from A.D. 1325 to 1475 were characterized by higher-than-average effective moisture, while the period from A.D. 1075 to 1325 was similar to the present (Weaver 1972: 44-45). These characterizations have been borne out to some degree by recent studies using data from sites along the Gila River and Queen Creek (Teague and Crown 1984); however, Weaver's model remains largely untested for the Salt River Valley, in part because few excavated sites give evidence of a continuous occupation from the Sedentary through the Classic periods. In this regard, the excavations at Las Colinas will provide an excellent opportunity for examining environmental changes throughout this portion of the sequence.

Research Topics and Data Requirements

We will thus address a single, general question: *what was the nature of the prehistoric natural environment and what changes in that environment may be documented during the occupation of the site*? The basic data with which this question will be addressed will come from the analyses of the pollen and flotation samples, wood charcoal, and faunal materials recovered from the site. These data will form the baseline for comparison and correlation with existing environmental data from other localities. Gathering data with which to properly address this question may be more difficult thn is generally thought; the results of Salt-Gila Aqueduct environmental studies (Fish 1984) indicate that the Hohokam so altered the environment surrounding their sites that it is almost impossible in some cases to determine the nature of the natural environment. In order to minimize this potential source of bias, it will be necessary to augment the site-specific environmental data which will be recovered during excavation.

Toward that end, in addition to the collection and analysis of materials from Las Colinas and AZ T:12:38 (ASM), existing literature pertaining to the geology, pedology, palynology, synecology, and ecology of the Salt River Valley will be synthesized and evaluated in an attempt to coordinate existing paleoenvironmental knowledge. Limited field checks of reported paleoenvironmental sites will be conducted, and potentially environmentally sensitive areas within the valley will be examined. Interpretation and correlation of data gathered during the Las Colinas excavation will be conducted by staff consultants; such an integrative, multidisciplinary approach should produce the greatest amount of information for the least investment of time and money. The following specific tasks have been defined.

1. Existing pollen and flotation data from the Salt River Valley and adjoining areas will be compiled.
2. Dendroclimatological data for all of Arizona will be compiled and compared with the palynological and macrofloral data base.
3. The ecology and distribution of native vegetation for the Salt River Valley will be evaluated as a means of

reconstructing, insofar as possible, plant community distributions and densities during the Hohokam occupation. This may include an examination of the historical records for the period from 1850 to about 1930, which marks the beginning of modern ubran growth and agricultural development.

4. The geological literature will be examined to determine: (a) the amount of downcutting and aggradation, the timing of such events, and, if possible, their initiating mechanism(s); and (b) the paleohydrologic characteristics of the river.

5. Existing soils literature will be evaluated in terms of: (a) the value of pedological information in paleoenvironmental reconstruction, (b) its possible use in chronology development, and (c) the limitations of specific soil types for agricultural purposes.

6. Existing groundwater literature will be examined to determine the relationship between local ecology and the water table.

7. Finally, the Las Colinas faunal assemblage will be compared to those from other sites in the Salt River Valley in order to explore the character of specific site environments.

Problem Domain II: Irrigation Technology

The Hohokam agricultural complex in the Salt River Valley is one of the most extensive prehistoric irrigation systems in the southwestern United States. Indeed, some canal segments within the system probably represent the remains of "the largest canals known from Precolumbian North America . . . " (Masse 1981: 408). The complete extent of this system is not known, but estimates of the total length of the main canals range from 125 miles (Halseth 1947) to 300 miles (Midvale 1966). Nicholas (1983) notes that definition problems prohibit an accurate determination of the extent of the system, but suggests that there may have been as many as 360 miles of main canals in the valley, based on reconstructions from previous studies and analysis of topographic maps. It should be noted that none of these estimates necessarily reflects the maximum extent of the Hohokam irrigation system, nor do they suggest contemporaneous use of the entire system.

The Hohokam were not unique in their ability to construct and maintain large irrigation systems; prehistoric irrigation systems of equal or greater magnitude are known from other continents. The extent and complexity of the system, however, imply the use of rather sophisticated surveying and construction methods. Although it is unlikely that we will ever be able to ascertain the details of their engineering methods, the Hohokam clearly possessed the expertise to establish and maintain grade on individual canals over 20 miles in length and appear to have understood the basic principles of flow dynamics.

The existence of this prehistoric irrigation system has been recognized for nearly 300 years. Captain Juan Mateo Manje and Father Eusebio Kino were apparently the first to describe the canals, in 1690 (Nicolas 1983). The first excavation of a Hohokam canal was conducted by Cushing in 1887 (Haury 1945) and Fewkes (1912) excavated several canals in the early 1900s. The canal systems had been extensively mapped by the 1920s (Turney 1924, 1929). Excavation of canals in the vicinity of Snaketown, conducted by Gladwin and others (1937), were followed by Woodbury''s excavations of prehistoric canals near Park of the Four Waters in Phoenix (Woodbury 1960). "By the mid-1960s, a total of seven or eight prehistoric canals had been tested . . . " (Masse 1976: 38). Over the last decade, prehistoric canals have been the subject of intensifying and increasingly systematic study. Herskovitz (1981) tested canals in the area of Tempe and Brooks conducted similar studies in the vicinity of Queen Creek (1975). Haury published information on canal studies carried out in 1964 and 1975 in conjunction with the Snaketown excavations (1976); these were followed by Crown's studies of prehistoric water control and conservation (1981b). The most comprehensive studies to date are those by Masse (1976) and Nicholas (1983). Only the more recent studies (since about 1965) have been conducted in a systematic fashion and have consistently recovered information beyond the presence, location, and gross dimensions of the canals.

Research Topics and Data Requirements

The study of prehistoric canals potentially provides a relatively unusual insight into anthropological questions about the prehistoric occupants of Las Colinas and other Hohokam sites in the Phoenix Basin. Among the potential information returns are: (1) insight on the organization of Hohokam society, (2) relationships of canals to principal occupation complexes, (3) a potential means of understanding the observed distribution of site complexes, (4) evaluation of the amount of potentially arable land available to the prehistoric occupants of the area, (5) approximations of the amount and organization of labor required for the construction and maintenance of the irrigation system, (6) techniques of water distribution, (7) modification of the landscape and soils as a result of irrigation, and (8) comparison with other prehistoric and historic irrigation systems. This list is by no means exhaustive and is intended solely as an indication of research directions. A variety of information returns will be sought during the proposed investigation of the canals associated with Las Colinas. For organizational purposes, the proposed study of the irrigation system will be separated into three broad topics: *the planning and construction of the canals*, *operation and maintenance of the system*, and *the dating of the canals.*

Planning and Construction of Canals

Numerous characteristics of the preshistoric canals imply planning and design. The canals increase in size and complexity from their beginnings during the Pioneer period to the later Classic period (Nicholas and Neitzel 1981). The canals have a grade steep enough to reduce sedimentation, yet shallow enough to prohibit downcutting. The observed distribution of major sites along the canal system (Gregory 1982) implies the planned location of sites, if not the canal system itself. The implications of the presence of the canal system for Hohokam sociopolitical organization have been discussed by Nicholas and Neitzel (1981). Although interpretations may vary from that of Nicholas and Neitzel, most investigators would agree that the extent and character of the canals suggest that they were predesigned, at least in part, and involved considerable cooperative effort among some portion of the Hohokam populace.

Canal construction activities may be divided into three categories: (1) disaggregation and dislocation of the sediment, (2) transport of the sediment to the canal embankment or to some other locus of deposition, and (3) disposal of the sediment. Most soils and sediments in the Salt River Valley are relatively unconsolidated and could be easily dislodged with digging sticks or stone hoes; however, P'w' notes "that the first attempt to construct a canal in the Phoenix area by modern man in December of 1867 resulted in failure as red-headed K. W. (Jack) Swilling began construction on the north bank of the Salt River in the hard caliche-cemented colluvium of Papago Pediment opposite the present location of downtown Tempe" (P'w' 1978: 8; see also Peplow 1970). One object of the proposed investigation is a compilation of soil and sediment types within the Phoenix Basin for correlation with the distribution of canal segments.

The dislodged sediment was probably removed (transported) using basketry, textile, or hide containers, although this is as yet unconfirmed. The use of ceramic containers, as in other primitive irrigation systems, seems unlikely. Excavation of canal embankments could conceivably reveal the size of individual loads and might indicate whether the sediment was wet or dry when removed. Deposition in most instances appears to have been immediately adjacent to the excavation and examination of intact embankments and excavated canal segments may confirm or deny this supposition. Unfortunately, most of the canal embankments have been obliterated (Masse 1976).

The total quantity of sediment removed in canal construction can be approximated by measuring canal cuts and the few remaining embankments. In addtion to its use in understanding the technology, this information might provide a more accurate means of estimating the labor required in canal construction. All the evidence necessary for such an estimation is not available from the Las Colinas study area; however, much can be learned from previously published information, particularly from studies conducted prior to extensive urban and agricultural development of the Phoenix area.

As previously noted, the Hohokam were capable of maintaining relatively consistent grades on the canals over long distances. Of the canals studied by Nicholas (1983), most had grades of from 2.0 to 10.0 feet per mile. Locally steeper grades of as much as 98.0 feet per mile are described by Masse (1976) but were apparently uncommon. The significance of grade is that grade controls the velocity of flow, which in turn controls the rate of infiltration loss, the deposition of sediment, vegetation growth, and the dimensions of the canal necessary to maintain a given rate of flow. A measure of the Hohokam understanding of flow dynamics could be obtained by examining the relationship between the grades of various canal segments and local substrate as shown on geologic and soil maps.

Another means of appraising the technological expertise of the Hohokam is through analysis of modifications of canal courses and profiles in accordance with varying topographic conditions, as a means of maintaining grade. Although a channel will adjust and develop its own grade to a certain extent, the maintenance of a consistent grade in areas of locally steepened topography generally requires course adjustment or modification of the canal cross section. Some modification of canal courses to preserve grade has been noted (Bandelier 1892), but no systematic study of the relationship between local slope and canal characteristics over large areas has been made.

Operation and Maintenance of the Canals

Geological investigations of the Las Colinas canal segments and of the irrigation system at large may provide insights into certain aspects of the operation and maintenance of the Hohokam irrigation system. Collecting this information will require extensive examination and correlation of existing archaeological, geological, pedological, and synecological literature, plus additional field studies in the Las Colinas area and the Phoenix Basin in general.

While all canals require periodic maintenance, the labor required for the operation and maintenance of any given portion of the canal and agricultural system is largely dependent upon the character of the canals (grade and the relationships among its width, depth, and length), the terrain across which the canals were constructed (substrate, paleotopography), the volume and periodicity of flow conducted by the canals, the nature of the lateral distribution system, and the local vegetation.

Maintenance could assume a variety of forms, depending upon the local conditions, including removal of organic matter and deposited sediments, repair of washed-out sections of the canal, and so forth. Unfortunately, much of the information necessary for a complete determination of maintenance techniques has been removed along with the canal embankments which stood in the way of modern agricultural practices and urbanization.

It appears that excess vegetation may have been cleared from the canals by burning (Bohrer 1971, Masse 1976). Whether or not this was a standard practice throughout the

Phoenix Basin has not been determined. The cleaning of excess sediments from the canals is even more problematic. The only means of assessing the extent of this practice is the examination of extant canal embankments throughout the basin. This will require field examination in areas beyond the limits of the Las Colinas I-10 corridor.

Loss of water through infiltration could have been a severe problem in some areas of the irrigation system, and several means of reducing those losses are possible. Canals may have been locally steepened to overcome the problem (which would probably have led to downcutting), or an impermiable lining may have been applied to the canals in some instances. Natural sedimentation of silt and clay in the canal bottom may have reduced the problem in some areas. Identifying the use of artificial linings in the canals is problematic; nonetheless, all available canal exposures should be examined for evidence of their presence.

Seepage loss from canals could lead to salinization or waterlogging of downslope areas adjacent to the canals. Historic agriculturalists in the area encountered these problems and it is reasonable to assume that prehistoric farmers also faced them. The potential extent of waterlogging and salinization should be considered in estimates of potentially arable land in prehsitoric times, although the entire area was probably never waterlogged at one time (Douglas 1938). Recognition of prehistoric problems of this sort are complicated because of historic agricultural and irrigation practices; however, waterlogging in the immediate vicinity of the canals in some areas is indicated by the presence of manganese oxides exposed in certain excavations (Masse 1976). Indirect evidence of such problems includes corrective measures such as drainage ditches. The distribution and extent of waterlogged and alkaline areas recognized by early Anglo settlers may indicate the potential extent of the problem, although such areas may have been produced by factors other than Hohokam irrigation practices (Schroeder 1940, 1943).

The operational efficiency and extent of the Hohokam irrigation system depended in part on the flow characteristics of the Salt River during the prehistoric occupation. The flow capacity of the irrigation system can be roughly approximated by examining the size, grade, and other characteristics of the canalf the prehistoric flow characteristics can be approximated, this information would provide a means of estimating how much of the system could have been in operation at one time. Paleoclimatic reconstructions will prove useful in estimating prehistoric river flow, as will analysis of alluvium deposited during the time in question. One objective of the canal study is the examination of alluvial deposits of the Salt River and correlation, if possible, with the prehistoric chronology.

Dating the Canals

Individual canals and channels within canals are imprecisely dated at the present time. The use of traditional methods—ceramic and radiocarbon dating—has allowed the broad temporal placement of some canals, but does not permit differentiation of use-episodes. Unfortunately, the dates assigned to Hohokam pottery are accurate only to the level of a hundred years or so. Radiocarbon dating is potentially more precise; however, several problems limit its effectiveness in dating canals. Previous archaeological investigations of sites and canals have produced only a limited number of radiocarbon samples in unquestionable stratigraphic context. In addition, the large standard deviations typical of radiocarbon dates of younger materials precludes separation of construction or use episodes that are not separated by a lengthy hiatus.

Archaeomagnetic dating has the potential to reduce these problems. Traditionally, this method involves assay of the paleomagnetic characteristics of sediments containing magnetic particles that have been heated, in place, above the Curie point. This method may be viable for some canal deposits because of the heating associated with a particular maintenance activity, the burning of brush in the canals. Evidence of such in situ burning was noted by Masse (1976).

A recently developed variation on this traditional method may be even more useful. Clay particles deposited from suspension in standing water have a statistical tendency to align themselves with the prevailing magnetic flux at the time of deposition. This tendency is measurable and its accuracy, according to Robert L. DuBois (University of Oklahoma), is theoretically comparable to traditional archaeomagnetic dating. Samples are collected in the same manner as heated-clay samples. Sediments within the canals and, if present, reservoirs will be sampled in a vertical column in an attempt to date preserved slack-water deposits within the canals and to determine a fill sequence within reservoirs.

Problem Domain III: The Hohokam Subsistence Base

The generalized models of Hohokam subsistence presented by past researchers have generally invoked the notion of stress as a prime determinant of Hohokam diet (Plog 1980; Upham and Rice 1980). Such studies suggest that the Hohokam used wild plant and animal resources in greater amounts as environmental changes, local degradation of the environment, and population pressure forced them to do so. Results from the Salt-Gila Aqueduct Project provide a more benign view of the relationship between man, environment, and diet from the Colonial through the Classic period (Teague and Crown 1981). Las Colinas, which was continuously occupied from at least as early as the Sacaton phase through the late Civano phase, provides an excellent laboratory for examining prehistoric subsistence. It should thus be possible to enumerate the range of species exploited during each phase of occupation, and to evaluate the relative importance of each to the Hohokam diet. Taken in concert with the information on the sociopolitical structure represented at Las Colinas, this should provide us with an important perspective on how closely subsistence was tied to both the local environmental conditions and the broader economic changes believed to have occurred during the occupation of the site.

Incipient Domestication

One new, emerging set of problems relating to the subsistence practices of the prehistoric Hohokam revolves around the possibility that at least two plant species—wild barley and agave—may have been husbanded or cultivated by the prehistoric populations. While there is little question that the Hohokam used these species (as evidenced by their occurrence in undisputed prehistoric contexts), the exploration of the nature of their use has only just begun in Hohokam studies. The problem of significance is the manner in which these plants were used and the impact of their use on the overall pattern of Hohokam economy and subsistence. The use of barley as a cultivated crop, for example, would have provided a greater degree of control over the foodstuffs available at given times of the year. The cultivation of barley, a winter and spring crop, would have freed them from reliance on stored or gathered wild foods which would otherwise have been necessary during those seasons. Agave is highly productive when cultivated and is easy to prepare and store; properly prepared, agave can last two to three years. Obviously, the advantages of having such a resource are great. In addition, the cultivation of both of these species would enhance the ability of groups to produce surpluses, potentially important with respect to exchange of both foodstuffs and other goods.

Presence of New Plant Varieties

Evidence from the Salt-Gila Aqueduct project sites suggests that new varieties of corn came into use among the Hohokam during the Classic period. According to Charles Miksicek, these varieties represent both Puebloan and Mexican types, providing information on a plausible new source of evidence regarding contact between these groups during the latter part of the Hohokam sequence. It will again be interesting to examine the sequence of varieties in use at Las Colinas, where the continuous use of the site from the Colonial through Classic periods should permit us to discern the time at which such varieties first came into use. These studies will also provide us with important information on the varieties in use in the Salt River Valley during the Classic period, in contrast to those in use in other areas of the Hohokam region.

The Role of Animal Resources

With a few recent exceptions (Teague and Crown 1981), little progress has been made in assessing the relative importance of animal species in Hohokam subsistence. The faunal materials recovered from Las Colinas, in concert with data available from other sites, should provide a basis for examining this question. The possibility of cross-cultural studies of the role of animal species in the subsistence base of agriculturalists in general is also a potentially interesting anthropological question with implications which obviously transcend Hohokam studies.

Nonfood Use of Plants

The Hohokam gathered and used a wide variety of plant species. Many of these had no apparent food value, and some have been recovered from contexts which provide definite evidence of nonfood uses, for example, as construction materials and firewood. An attempt will be made to define the patterns of nonfood plant use at Las Colinas and to document how and why these patterns may have changed through time.

Research Questions and Data Requirements

In addition to identifying the range of plant and animal species represented at the site, a number of basic issues may be examined, including incipient domestication of wild plant foods and the introduction of new varieties. The abundance and kinds of plant remains, as well as their distribution, may reflect certain aspects of social organization, such as the production of surplusses for exchange or the control of certain species by hypothesized elite groups. Finally, the distribution of animal bone, and its abundance relative to plant remains, may be indicative of the relative importance of these foods in the prehistoric diet. The following questions will guide research along these lines.

1. *Is there evidence of differential access to foodstuffs at Las Colinas?* One expression of the postulated social differentiation of Hohokam society during the Classic and possibly the Sedentary period may be differential access to foodstuffs. This question may be addressed by plotting the distribution of the remains of foodstuffs in contemporaneous contexts across the site and comparing those distributions with evidence of social differentiation in other data classes. It will also be useful to examine the different foods represented by remains from various contexts at Las Colinas and the contemporary contexts (if any) AZ T:12:38 (ASM).

2. *Is there evidence of surplus production and exchange of foodstuffs?* Because the intrusive nature of particular plant or animal species is often impossible to determine, this topic is difficult to address, and must be approached indirectly. Through the functional evaluation of features and structures, it may be possible to assess the potential

volume of available storage facilities at any given time. In addition, it should be possible to estimate the amount of land in the site area that could have been devoted to fields. The abundance of specific artifact types (spindle whorls or mescal knives, for example) may indicate the processing of plant materials in greater amounts than could be expected for localized use. Particular species may occur at the site in frequencies suggestive of surplus production. Finally, evidence for suprahousehold group processing and production may be found in the presence of particular feature types such as hornos, which may have been used by groups larger than the household (Wilcox and Sternberg 1981).

3. *Is there evidence of incipient domestication of particular species by the Hohokam at Las Colinas?* The relative abundance of plant species other than known cultigens, as well as changes in the morphology of those species, may be indicative of their domestication.

4. *Is there evidence of the introduction of new varieties of domesticates during the Classic period?* Using the basic inventory of plant species through time, the sequence of varieties of corn used at Las Colinas may be identified and the appearance of new varieties may be dated.

5. *What was the role of animal resources in the Hohokam subsistence base?* In addition to identifying the range of animal species represented at Las Colinas, it should be possible to quantify the relative importance of these species in the diet and to document changes in the pattern of animal resource use which may have occurred through time. The possibility that social differentiation may be reflected in differential access to animal resources will be explored under Question 1. Finally, the faunal assemblage from Las Colinas will be compared with contemporaneous samples from other sites, to determine whether the use of animal resources differed across geographic space or among site types.

6. *What nonfood uses of plant species were practiced by the Hohokam?* The range of plant species used for purposes other than food (as construction materials, firewood, and so forth) will be identified. Of special interest is the documentation of patterns of wood use and consumption, and possible changes in its availability through time.

Chapter 4

AZ T:12:38 (ASM): BACKGROUND, PROBLEM DOMAINS, RESEARCH QUESTIONS, AND DATA REQUIREMENTS

The following section of the proposal deals with the site designated AZ T:12:38 (ASM) and is divided into three parts. The first section summarizes the information collected during the testing program conducted at the site and provides a review and assessment of the characteristics of the site. The second section deals with several additional considerations that are not covered in the testing report but are relevant to the research potential of the site. In the third section, potential research problems are presented and data required to address them are described.

Background and Previous Research

AZ T:12:38 (ASM) was originally recorded in 1978 during a survey of the I-10 corridor by personnel from the Arizona State Museum. The site was recorded as two distinct, low mounds that had been cut by Moreland Avenue on the south, and an associated artifact scatter which extended to the north away from Moreland Avenue (Fig. 4.1). This scatter was recorded as covering an area approximately 65 m north-south by 100 m east-west. Also noted was an historic canal or ditch remnant in the eastern portion of the site (Arizona State Museum Site Survey Files).

In 1979 the Museum of Northern Arizona conducted test excavations at the site, which was designated NA15,790 in the site recording system of that institution. The results of the testing program have been reported by Yablon (1980). This report indicates that the testing included a total of eight backhoe trenches in the immediate area of the site and the controlled machine stripping of an area described in the report as measuring 30 m by 45 m (Yablon 1980: 37). This description does not agree with the size of the tested area shown on the maps of the site included in the testing report, which, according to the scale indicated, measures approximately 27 m east-west by 60 m north-south (Yablon 1980, Figs. 15 and 18). The reasons for this apparent discrepancy are unclear, although it may be nothing more than a typographical error.

Machine stripping was carried to a depth of 1.25 m below the present ground surface, and resulted in the discovery and hand excavation of 10 prehistoric features. These features included a poorly preserved pit house, a cremation, an extended inhumation, six pits, and an ash-filled depression. The trash area noted by the original survey and located along the southern margin of the right-of-way was not given a feature number, and it unclear whether this deposit was removed by hand excavation or machine stripping. The low number of artifacts recovered from the purported trash area (48 sherds, 6 lithics) is inconsistent with its identification as refuse. Further, it is unclear whether all of this deposit was removed during the testing. The map shown in Figure 15 (Yablon 1980) indicates that, because the "trash area" lay entirely within the area that was machine stripped, it would have been completely removed. In the absence of profiles and other supporting data, it is impossible to determine from the report whether any of this deposit is extant.

The single pit house, the inhumation, and one of the pits (Feature 4) produced Santa Cruz phase ceramic material, while the trash deposit at the southern margin of the right-of-way produced materials indicating a Classic period date (Yablon 1980: 48). It should be noted that the Santa Cruz phase material in the burial pit may represent redeposited material and does not necessarily date the burial itself (Yablon 1980: 48). The cremation produced no datable ceramics.

As was noted in the original survey description and reiterated in the testing report, the former extent of the site is unknown. The remainder of the site area apparently lies to the south of the freeway corridor and has been covered by a trailer court and possibly other residences. The northern margin of the site appears to fall within the corridor, and corresponds roughly to the extent of the artifact scatter noted during the original survey.

In sum, the available information suggests that the remains designated AZ T:12:38 (ASM) represent the northern edge of a site of unknown size, and that the site witnessed at least two periods of occupation: a Santa Cruz phase, Colonial period occupation represented by at least one pit house and probably other features, and a Classic period occupation of undetermined phase, represented by a trash deposit and possibly other features.

While the nature of any remaining Classic period features and deposits is difficult to predict, more may be said concerning the probable character of the Santa Cruz phase occupation.

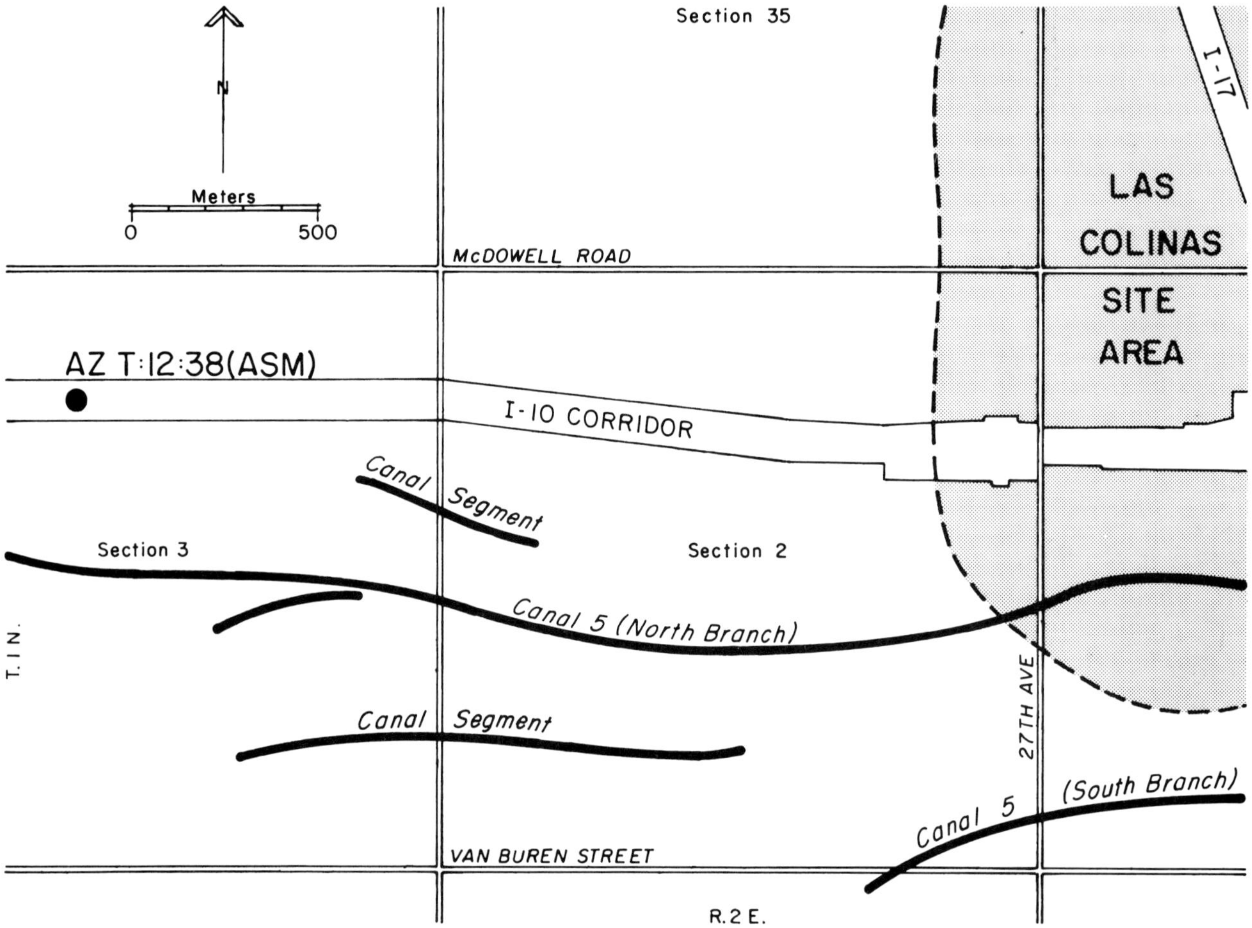

Figure 4.1. The location of AZ T:12:38 (ASM) relative to Las Colinas and major canals in the area.

As noted above, the entryway of the single house excavated during the testing program was not discovered; however, the long axis of the house has a north-south orientation. Haury (1976) notes that the doorway is located approximately in the center of one of the long walls in most Colonial period pit houses. Thus, it is likely that the entry to this structure faced either east or west. In their recent consideration of the Snaketown data, Wilcox and others have shown that eastward and southward doorway orientations predominate among Santa Cruz phase houses (Wilcox and others 1981: 162). Assuming that this pattern holds true at AZ T:12:38 (ASM) and that the doorway was indeed on the long axis of the house, the entryway probably opened to the east, then any associated houses, extramural features, or both, would probably be found in the area east of the house. The house itself is located very near the eastern margin of the tested area, and there is sufficient space between that area and the nearest backhoe trench to the east to accomodate a number of houses and other features (Yablon 1980, Fig. 15). Thus, if additional Santa Cruz features exist, this is the area in which they will most likely be located.

Additional Considerations

Several additional observations may be made concerning AZ T:12:38 (ASM) which are relevant to an assessment of the research potential of the site and the data recovery proposed below. These observations deal with: (1) the stratigraphic position of the prehistoric deposits, (2) the significance of the historic canal or ditch segment reported by the initial survey, and (3) the location of the site and its relationship to Las Colinas.

Site Stratigraphy

The testing program has established that the stratigraphy of the site area is composed of three levels. The uppermost unit is described as a "highly disturbed root zone," averaging 30 cm to 40 cm in thickness and sometimes containing historic trash (Yablon 1980: 37). This disturbed unit overlies a thick unit of alluvial deposits, probably silt, that contains occasional pockets of sand and gravel. This alluvial unit extended to the bottom of the backhoe trenches in most cases, or approximately 1.20 m to 1.30 m below the present ground surface (Yablon 1980: 20). Caliche encountered in the bottoms of some trenches constitutes a third stratum of unknown and probably variable thickness.

The upper, disturbed root zone is clearly a plow zone (Yablon 1980: 34). Historic records show that the quarter-section in which the site is located was first brought under cultivation in 1878 (Kent 1910), and aerial photographs indicate that the area was still under cultivation as late as 1963. Thus the postoccupational use-history and overall stratigraphy are similar to those documented for much of the Las Colinas site area (Gregory and McGuire 1982; Schreiber and others 1981), and it may be expected that the same general relationships between the natural and historic cultural stratigraphy and any prehistoric features and deposits will obtain at AZ T:12:38 (ASM). That is, features that were on or near the surface when cultivation began will have been substantially disturbed or completely destroyed. Features and deposits that have survived plowing will most often be encountered at the base of or immediately below the plow zone, at a depth of approximately 40 cm to 50 cm below the present ground surface.

The depths of the features documented during the testing program support this general interpretation. Features 1 through 6 appear to have been intruded from approximately the same surface, which would have been at the base of or slightly below the present plow zone. The destructive effects of plowing may account for the fragmentary nature and generally poor condition of the single pit house excavated during testing, and perhaps for the failure to discover a hearth or entryway associated with that feature (Yablon 1980: 42, 44). The remaining features were encountered at greater depths, but in the absence of additional supporting evidence, it is unlikely that deeply buried living surfaces are present at the site. Interestingly, the most well defined features—the pit house, the cremation, the pit beneath the pit house, and probably the inhumation—were encountered at shallower levels. This suggests that the other features may have gone unrecognized during machine stripping until their deeper and better defined portions were encountered. It may thus be expected that the remaining features at the site will be encountered at the base of or slightly below the plow zone. Machine stripping below the plow zone may obscure the outlines of features in the horizontal exposures produced; hand stripping, beginning immediately above the base of the plow zone, would be more prudent.

Historic Canal or Ditch Segment

As noted above, the initial survey record of the site shows a historic ditch or canal remnant in the site area. Although this feature is not mentioned in the testing report, it may be represented by a dip in the composite north-south profile of the site area illustrated in the report (Yablon 1980, Fig. 18). An awareness of its presence is important in the interpretation of environmental samples which may be recovered. For example, the cattail pollen *Typha domingensis* recovered from one of the samples taken during the testing and interpreted as being prehistoric in origin, may represent recent vegetation associated with the environment surrounding the historic ditch. Recognition of this historic feature is clearly important in interpreting any environmental samples recovered from the site, and may be important in interpreting the stratigraphy in particular areas of the site.

The Relationship of AZ T:12:38 (ASM) to Las Colinas

A previously unappreciated fact about AZ T:23:38 (ASM) is its proximity to and potential relationship with Las Colinas. Situated only some 2 kilometers to the west of Mound 8, the site would also have been located on or near the large Canal No. 5 or Canal Colinas (Fig. 4.1; Turney 1929), which also served Las Colinas.

Although the extent of the Classic period occupation at AZ T:12:38 (ASM) is unknown, it is clear that the site did not approach the size of Las Colinas, and there is no evidence that either a platform mound or a ballcourt ever existed at this site. Unless vegetation obscured the line of sight, the large Mound 7 and possibly several of the other major mounds at Las Colinas would probably have been visible from AZ T:12:38 (ASM). Given these observations and the obvious importance of Las Colinas as a major Classic period site, it is not unwarranted to suggest that the Classic period occupation at AZ T:12:38 (ASM) represented an "outlying" segment of the larger community. Consequently, depending upon the character of any remaining Classic period features and deposits at the site, comparative data relating to the research problems to be addressed at Las Colinas may be forthcoming from AZ T:12:38 (ASM).

With respect to the Santa Cruz phase occupation, the possible presence of one or more house clusters would suggest comparisons with contemporaneous materials that may be recovered from Las Colinas, and might shed light on the nature of Colonial period occupations in areas well away from the river, the nature of Colonial period social groups, and so on. If Santa Cruz phase house clusters are present at both sites, for example, they would constitute analytic units to be used in a variety of comparisons.

Research Questions and Data Requirements

Based on the results of the testing program, Yablon has suggested the following three research topics which might be investigated at AZ T:12:38 (ASM).

1. The role that mid-sized sites such as NA 15,790 played in the socioeconomic system of the Hohokam;

2. The internal patterning of mid-sized Hohokam sites;

3. Differential methods of disposal of the dead at mid-sized Hohokam sites (Yablon 1980: 50).

The usefulness and feasibility of these research topics must be questioned on several grounds. First, it is not at all certain that a "mid-sized" site is represented, as its full extent is unknown. Yablon noted that "it is impossible to determine the extent of the remains lying beneath the trailer court" (1980: 50). Further, such a focus does not take into account the fact that the size and character of the site may not have remained constant over time. Similar sampling problems may be cited with reference to an examination of the internal patterning of the site itself. Any inferences of site-level patterning would automatically be suspect because the portion of the site within the corridor is unknown and because of the presence of at least two components at the site. Finally, only two burials were recovered during the testing program, despite the fact that a substantial area was tested. It is unlikely that further work at the site will produce a burial population of sufficient size to address questions dealing with variability in burial practices; even the two burials thus far recovered may not have been deposited during the same period.

Given these criticisms and the information about the site presented above, several basic research questions better suited to the characteristics of the site as they are known at present may be suggested. The most fundamental issues at AZ T:12:38 (ASM) are practical ones concerning the numbers and kinds of features present and their distributions.

The overall research potential of AZ T:12:38 (ASM), as well as the appropriate research problems to be addressed, will be determined largely by the nature of the remains which are discovered there. The research problems to be addressed at Las Colinas will provide the principal context for the interpretation of the data obtained from AZ T:12:38 (ASM), and, in general, much of the research potential of the site lies in the fact that it may provide comparative data for use in conjunction with the research to be carried out at Las Colinas. Individual features or classes of features may serve as appropriate units of analysis and comparison. Comparative data on particular artifact classes, such as samples of specific ceramic types, may also be obtained from AZ T:12:38 (ASM) and will be examined in detail.

The following basic research questions have been proposed.

1. *What subsurface features and deposits exist at the site?*

2. *What is the spatial and temporal distribution of those features and deposits?*

   The answers to these questions will largely determine the further research potential of the site, and will be gained through the use of basic discovery techniques. Depending on the nature of additional features and deposits discovered, the following research questions may be addressed.

   If one or more Santa Cruz phase house groups are discovered at AZ T:12:38 (ASM):

3. *What are the characteristics of the house groups at AZ T:12:38 (ASM)? How do they compare with those recorded at Las Colinas and with those documented at other sites such as Snaketown?*

4. *What may be inferred about the size and composition of the social units represented by the house groups at the site? How do these compare with inferences derived from contemporaneous groups at Las Colinas and other sites?*

5. *What subsistence activities were carried out in conjunction with the occupation of the site? How do these compare with those inferred for the contemporaneous occupation at Las Colinas and at other sites?*

   If partially intact Classic period trash deposits are discovered at AZ T:12:38 (ASM):

6. *How does the content of these refuse deposits compare with similar deposits from the central area of Las Colinas? Are artifact classes and floral and faunal remains, differentially represented in deposits from the two sites?*

7. *What do these comparisons indicate about the similarities or differences in life in the central area of a major site and in an outlying but nearby settlement?*

Chapter 5

DATA RECOVERY AND ANALYSIS STRATEGIES

Las Colinas

The data recovery strategies appropriate to Las Colinas are determined by the nature of the problems to be addressed. An emphasis on site structure and temporal and spatial evidence of organizational differentiation dictates that, in addition to specific features targeted for investigation (such as Mound 8 and the canals), the excavation strategy should produce broad horizontal exposures so that spatial relationships between features and deposits may be examined, and so that distributional studies of the artifacts recovered may be undertaken. Sampling of space may provide a general characterization of the nature of remains within defined areas, but does not permit adequate definition of site structure for the stated research purposes. Therefore, the proposed excavation strategy includes concentration of exposures in Areas 3, 4, and 5, and in the western end of Area 1, where intact evidence of site structure is expected.

Analysis strategies proposed here similarly emphasize efforts to define both internal differentiation and change through time in the nature of that differentiation, through subsistence-related sampling as well as the investigation of material culture assemblages. Subsequent interpretation will relate this to other sites and other areas, but first a firm grasp of variability within Las Colinas itself is required.

General Excavation Methods

In general, site excavation will follow the procedures outlined in the Cultural Resource Management Division Excavation Manual (Teague 1979); only a brief review of these procedures in terms of strategies specific to Las Colinas will be presented here.

The entire corridor area will be gridded in 10-m-by-10-m units oriented to the cardinal directions. Vertical control will be maintained through use of the datum established in 1968 and still in place to the west of Mound 8 (elevation 1078.7 feet above sea level).

In all of those areas targeted for stripping (see below), the bulk of the plow zone will be removed with a front-end loader or other appropriate heavy equipment; a road grader or paddle-wheel scraper may be called for in some situations. Because the depth of the plow zone is well documented for the entire site area, this procedure may be accomplished without damage to the underlying features and deposits. Depending upon whether or not the area has been trenched, as well as other circumstances, a backhoe will then be used to dig trenches at systematic intervals across the stripped area. This will allow rapid discovery of features and will provide starting points for the horizontal exposure of the areas by hand. The order in which the machine stripping and trenching are accomplished may be reversed when necessary to avoid the unnecessary stripping of areas without features. Beginning with areas surrounding known features, the remaining plow zone will be stripped by hand in 5-m-by-5-m or 10-m-by-10-m units, while excavation of known features proceeds in 2-m-by-2-m units.

It should be noted that statistical extrapolation from trenching results will not be used to infer aspects of localized site structure, except at very general levels. Such approaches, to be sufficiently accurate for use in detailed projections, require intensive compensation for the exceedingly nonrandom and nonnormal distribution of features within Hohokam habitation sites. Given the current limitations of our data base, such compensations are not feasible at the necessary level of detail. Attempts to statistically predict feature distributions or densities without considering these structural variables have too often resulted in grossly exaggerated estimates. Attempts to define these variables must necessarily assume a broad regional uniformity in detailed characteristics of site structure; such uniformity has not been demonstrated and in fact should be under investigation rather than assumed at the Papago Freeway sites. We must therefore propose stripping of broad areas as the only feasible approach to definition of site structure at Las Colinas.

In two areas, more specific data recovery procedures may be outlined at this time.

In Area 6, which was unavailable for testing in 1980, a systematically placed series of trenches will be excavated, beginning at the eastern end nearest Area 5, where subsurface features and deposits are known to exist.

In Area 3, the area surrounding Mound 8, data recovery will begin with the removal of the 1968 excavation backdirt, and relocation of trenches excavated during the 1968 field season. The old excavations will then be cleared out and features that were only partially excavated in 1968 will be completely excavated. In addition, a systematic search will be made for historic features of potential significance. Finally, through hand trenching, a search will be made for additional features beneath the mound; any that are found will be excavated.

Excavation of Specific Features

It may be anticipated that a variety of features will be encountered during the course of the excavations, including trash pits, roasting pits, caliche puddling pits, houses, hornos, cremations, inhumations, and so forth. The numbers of features to be excavated and the completeness of excavation of features in each class will depend on the position of such features within the site and their relationship to other features; however, several general guidelines may be established with respect to particular feature classes. Trash pits and caliche puddling pits will be predictably numerous and it is clearly unnecessary to excavate each one of them. In the case of these features, a sufficient portion of them will be excavated to produce: (1) the necessary environmental samples, (2) a plan view and profile through some portion of the feature and a reasonable estimate of volume, and, where relevant, (3) a sufficient quantity of ceramic material for purposes of dating the feature, and (4) a representative sample of all classes of artifacts. If stratified trash deposits are encountered, they will, of course, be excavated in accordance with the stratigraphy present. Otherwise, arbitrary 10-cm levels will be used. All cremations and inhumations will be completely excavated. All houses will be completely excavated if possible; if it becomes necessary to sample houses, our efforts will be directed toward determining the size and orientation of the house and at obtaining samples for archaeomagnetic dating. Priority for full excavation will be given to those houses that burned in use or that, for other reasons, appear likely to provide the greatest interpretive potential.

Sequence of Excavation

Because most of the very large Area 6 was unavailable for testing, and because the testing of Area 4 was discontinued after two trenches in the very western end encountered subsurface features, the sequence of excavation at the site will be extremely important. It is necessary to insure that no surprises are in store in the less well known areas.

At the start of the fieldwork, one crew will begin work in the area around Mound 8 and another in the untested portions of Area 4. Two crew members will be assigned to monitor trenching in Area 6 at the same time, beginning in the eastern end nearest Area 5, where a high density of subsurface features and deposits is known to exist. In this way, the less well known areas of the corridor (4 and 6) may be assessed, and necessary adjustments to the field schedule made soon after the start of fieldwork. Assuming that current expectations are correct—that is, that there will be little or no material in most of Area 6 and a roughly continuous distribution of features and deposits in Area 4—the sequence of excavation will be as follows:

Crew 1	AZ T:12:38 (ASM); Las Colinas, Area 1; Las Colinas, Area 5
Crew 2	Las Colinas Areas 3 and 6
Crew 3	Las Colinas, Areas 4 and 6
Crew 4	Canal study

Backdirt Removal

Tremendous quantities of dirt will be produced by the machine removal of the plow zone in various areas and by the subsequent hand excavation of various features and deposits; the problem of removing it will be dealt with in several ways. First, a general plan of the sequence of work in the corridor area has been devised. While this plan necessarily subject to change, it provides a basic framework out of which the actual field decisions may evolve. Second, it is assumed that by the time large amounts of dirt are being moved, several areas within the corridor will have been tested and shown to contain no cultural features and thus cleared for the deposition of backdirt. As it is stripped, soil from plow zone will be placed in dump trucks and carted to these designated areas, keeping crossings of 27th Street to a minimum. Backdirt resulting from hand excavations will be deposited in designated areas for periodic removal by loader and dump truck at appropriate intervals. In this way, the removal of backdirt from hand excavations can be efficiently coordinated with the plow zone removal to minimize time and costs.

Artifact Analyses

The purposes and goals of the analyses of artifacts recovered from Las Colinas are threefold: (1) to produce an inventory of the materials and a basis for the presentation of descriptive data; (2) to provide a basis for distributional studies of the various artifact classes that relate to the research questions outlined above; and (3) to produce information concerning the characteristics of individual artifact classes as they relate to the research problems outlined above and to additional research problems that may be defined in the course of the project. Some of the problems relating to the ceramic assemblage are outlined below; additional research topics dealing specifically with other artifact classes may be defined as the project proceeds and as the nature of the sample of a given artifact class becomes apparent.

General Procedures

The intital washing and sorting of artifacts will be carried out in the field laboratory, which will function for the duration of the fieldwork. The artifacts will then be moved to Tucson, where the more detailed analyses will be conducted. General laboratory procedures for processing and basic analyses will follow those outlined in the Cultural Resource Management Division Analysis Manual (Wells 1982).

Ceramic Analysis

While the Hohokam ceramic typology has been in general use for many years (Haury 1937, 1976), the study and understanding of Hohokam ceramic manufacture has lagged far behind those of equivalent wares in the Anasazi and Mogollon areas. The reasons for this are simple: many fewer Hohokam sites have been excavated, and, in general, Hohokam ceramics have been viewed as a unified tradition, both stylistically and technologically, in a way that their northern counterparts have not. Nevertheless, in the last decade, the image of a unified tradition has been questioned with increasing frequency (Masse 1979; Neitzel 1982). Studies of Hohokam ceramic variability should have two basic functions: (1) to inform on the manufacture of the ceramics as artifacts, and (2) to inform on the manufacturers of the ceramics. The study of the Las Colinas assemblage will do both of these things, providing information for the assessement of three of the problem domains and research questions outlined above.

Chronology

In the absence of other reliable dating techniques for Hohokam sites, ceramics have come to play an increasingly important role in the temporal placement of features and sites. Although there have been arguments over the dating of the early end of the Hohokam sequence (Plog 1980; Schiffer 1982), the types indicative of the Sedentary and Classic periods are generally viewed as reliable chronological markers. Because these artifacts constitute our most effective temporal indicators, it has become crucial to discern all attributes—stylistic, formal, or technological—that appear to be temporally sensitive.

In the study of the Las Colinas assemblage from the 1968 excavations, Crown (1981a) found that temper type, even when defined on a gross level, was a temporally sensitive attribute of Hohokam ceramics at this site. This fact may be extremely useful in interpreting the features excavated during the 1982-1983 field season. By combining the analysis of traditional types with temper types, it may thus be possible to date features at a much finer level than the phase. It is expected that the preliminary dating of features and deposits on the basis of ceramic assemblages will be accomplished in the field laboratory. Thus, by the time fieldwork is completed, a preliminary temporal ordering of excavated features and deposits will be in hand, and will provide the basis for selection of, for example, the initial sets of pollen and flotation samples to be analyzed.

Ceramic Manufacture

While the shift in temper types and stylistic forms may be used to interpret the temporal sequence of features at the site, they may also be used to interpret shifts in manufacturing traditions. The change through time from schist-tempered to sand-tempered ceramics is an interesting phenomenon in itself. It may indicate one of several things: a gradual shift in the pottery-making tradition at Las Colinas, in the locus of manufacture of the pottery at Las Colinas, or in the personnel involved in pottery making. Obviously, understanding the causes for this change through time is important for an overall understanding of the Hohokam cultural tradition.

If this shift in technology is taken in concert with the shifts in stylistics and formal attributes of Hohokam ceramics, it may be possible to gain a greater understanding of the nature of the Sedentary- Classic period transition. In particular, it has been suggested that Hohokam ceramics (at least certain types) were "mass produced" by specialists during the Sedentary period (Haury 1976; Masse 1979). Such a tradition was both preceded and followed by localized production of ceramics by "amateurs". Such a drastic shift in manufacturing practices should certainly be apparent in the assemblage, particularly when the Sacaton and Soho phases are represented in the assemblage from a single site. If this change did indeed take place, the assemblage from Las Colinas will provide a rare opportunity to examine the nature of ceramic manufacture through time at a single site. The fact that a shift in one technological attribute (temper) is already recognized in the assemblage from the site suggests that further study will be successful in explaining this one aspect of the Sedentary-Classic period transition.

In addition, such studies may illuminate some of the changes that took place throughout the Classic period. The fact that the technological shifts found in the earlier study were continuous, but gradual, suggests that the shift in the manufacturing tradition was also gradual. But changes in design styles and changes in other aspects of the Hohokam tradition were apparently not so gradual. Further examination of this phenomenon should provide us with some insight into the ways in which the manufacture of these artifacts influenced and was influenced by the socioeconomic conditions of the Classic period.

Trade, Exchange, and Subregional Variability

While an understanding of the manufacture and use of ceramics at Las Colinas is of some importance to our understanding of the cultural processes at work during the

Sedentary and Classic periods, an understanding of the origins and presence of ceramics produced elsewhere is of equal importance to our understanding of the place of the site in the Hohokam regional system. For this reason identifying both the context and origin, at least in general terms, of intrusive ceramics is of considerable value. Both vessels and their contents may have been exchanged; in either event, such exchange tied the occupants of this site to other sites and other areas.

While ceramics have tremendous importance for the interpretation of the events of occupation at Las Colinas, they must first be interpreted themselves. Many attributes visible to the naked eye may be recorded and analyzed to provide information sufficient to answer many questions; however, questions involving locus of manufacture generally require more detailed technological analyses. Crown's (1981a) recognition of at least one microtradition at the site provides important corroboration for the in-place manufacture of some of the assemblage. Additional information provides equally strong corroboration for the nonlocal manufacture of other components of the assemblage, even if within the Hohokam region. It thus becomes crucial to test the validity of our identification of local versus nonlocal manufacture through more detailed analyses.

Different types of technological analyses will be useful for exploring particular problems. Fundamental to any study of the Las Colinas material will be the initial analysis of the assemblage, followed by further structuring of the problems which may be addressed using that assemblage, and the selection of a sample for detailed technological analysis. It is thus impossible to provide a precise explication of which sherds would undergo which tests at this juncture; however, given the range of techniques available for such analyses, it is possible to evaluate their utility in addressing the general problem areas outlined above. Petrographic analysis is easily performed and provides detailed information on nonplastic constituents of ceramics, both by type and frequency. For more detailed understanding of production locus, emission spectroscopy (which measures major elements in the clay) may be useful, as well as the yet more precise atomic absorption (which measures the concentrations of elements in parts per million). These two chemical analyses may also be useful for distinguishing the paint and slip types used.

Lithic Anlaysis

Hohokam lithic assemblages generally do not repay intensive technological study. Functional studies, however, may be useful in several interpretive contexts, including the study of subsistence practices. Identification of material sources contributes to the investigation of areal and regional interrelationships. Initially, the Las Colinas assemblage will be sorted into basic technological classes, recording material types and selecting samples for more detailed functional analyses. The specific directions to be taken by those analyses will depend upon the character of the lithic assemblages recovered, as assessed by the basic inventory, and will be determined after the fieldwork is completed.

Shell Analysis

The study of shell assemblages is productive in addressing problems of regional interaction and of the role of individual communities in that interaction, as well as in the investigation of social differentiation within sites. Sorting the Las Colinas shell on the basis of artifact type and species represented will provide the data on which distributional studies may be based. These, in turn, may support inferences concerning possible status differentiation among the occupants of the site. For example, was there standardization in the production of shell artifacts; if so, how does it vary through time? What changes occur over time in the source(s) of shell? How did specific classes of shell artifacts function? Were some artifacts available to the entire population, while the use of others was restricted to certain groups? Depending upon the nature of the sample recovered, additional research problems may be designed specifically around the shell assemblage.

Pollen, Flotation, Wood Charcoal, and Faunal Samples

The collection of pollen and flotation samples, wood charcoal, and faunal remains will be of central importance to the environmental and subsistence studies outlined in Chapter 3 and the research questions dealing specifically with these materials are discussed there. The information recovered from these samples will also be important to a number of the site-specific research questions outlined in Chapter 2. The specific guidelines for the recovery of these materials are presented here.

A large number of pollen and flotation samples will be taken from a variety of contexts. Because plans call for sampling all reliable contexts, and because we wish to produce a carefuly time- ordered sequence of samples, pollen and flotation samples will not be selected for analysis until excavation is complete. At that time, samples deemed appropriate to the research problems outlined above will be chosen from the most reliable temporal and cultural contexts.

Pollen and flotation samples from cultural contexts will be collected in accordance with the guidelines presented in Table 5.1 (adapted from Fish and Miksicek 1982: 169-173). Pollen samples will also be taken from sterile levels beneath the occupation surface(s). Historic features will be sampled in order to evaluate postoccupational environmental changes.

The analysis of flotation materials will include wood charcoal in addition to items such as seeds. To supplement the flotation samples, wood charcoal encountered during screening will also be collected; all specimens thus recovered from critical proveniences such as features and occupation surfaces

Table 5.1

Guidelines for Pollen and Flotation Sampling

Provenience	*Pollen*	*Flotation*
Architectural Features		
Pit house interiors	sample each half of floor	same
	sample between floor and roof fall	sample roof fall, including fragments of beams and covering material
	sample above roof	same
	sample under in-place artifacts on floor	not necessary
	do not sample hearth, but hearth fill	collect as much of nearby surface as possible
	sample floor features suggesting specialized	sample floor contact immediately around hearth
	activity	or other areas with obviously burned material
Pit house exteriors	sample occupation surface outside door	same (if carbon present)
	sample any apparent specialized activity loci	same (if carbon present)
Ramadas	sample floor (each quadrant)	same
	sample activity areas (such same as pot breaks)	same
	avoid hearth	sample the fill of interior or exterior hearths
	sample occupation surface adjacent to hearth	same
Surface adobe structures	treat same as pit houses or ramadas	same
	sample definable surface on which the adobe wall was built	not necessary
Plazas	sample occupation surface at intervals appropriate to size of exposed area, with special attention to activity loci	sample activity areas with obvious burned material
Specialized Features		
Trash mounds	if no stratigraphy is apparent sample several different points horizontally and vertically	same
	if stratigraphy is visible, sample individual horizons or "basket loads"	same
Burials	sample fill of burial pit in the thoracic region	same (carbonized material will probably not be associated)
	sample the bottom contact zone of the fill of burial vessels	sample the vessel fill only if the fill has been charred
Cremations	ignore	for secondary deposites, sample the urn (bone and accompanying artifacts will be saved)
		for primary cremations (a body on a pyre) sample any obvious strata
Roasting pits	sample of fill near bottom	as much of fill as possible
	if there are several obvious use episodes, sample separately	same
	sample external occupation surface	sample only of carbonized material is visible
	sample under rocks sealing the pit	not necessary

Table 5.1 (continued)

Guidelines for Pollen and Flotation Sampling

Provenience	*Pollen*	*Flotation*
Storage pits	sample bottom contact zone	sample bottom fill only if contents are burned
	sample quadrants in very large pits	
	sample generalized fill	
Isolated hearths	sample exterior occupation surface (only if buried; avoid surface hearths)	sample only if carbonized materials are apparent
	ignore ashy fill	collect as much of fill as possible
Artifacts		
Ground stone in primary context	leave as much dirt on grinding surface as seal in *clean* plastic bag; label "Do Not Wash"; send to lab	ignore
Whole vessels	clean out most of matrix, then sample bottom contaxt zone	save entire fill if contents are burned; otherwise ignore

will be analyzed. The heavy fraction of analyzed flotation samples will be saved and all artifacts and faunal materials recovered, along with provenience data, will be submitted to appropriate analysts for study.

All animal bone recovered during excavation will be analyzed. Feature fill will be sifted through one-quarter-inch mesh to maximize recovery of bone. An adequate sample of very small bone, which might not be recovered by this process, should be obtained from the flotation samples.

Canal Study

The investigation of the Hohokam canal systems will focus first on the canal segments associated with Las Colinas. The data collected from these features will be analyzed and interpreted, and will be augmented by the synthesis of existing data relating to the prehistoric canal systems of which they were a part. These comparative and synthetic studies must rely heavily on examination of previously published literature pertaining to the geology, pedology, ecology, and archaeology of the area. Although these studies will derive information on the canals from other areas, the information pertains directly to Las Colinas, because the irrigation canals functioned as a *system*, in which no single component can be isolated from all others.

Methods

Our investigation of the Las Colinas canal segments will include the following program of research.

First, canal segments exposed during the testing program will be reexcavated and sediment samples will be taken from those canal segments for purposes of determining paleohydrological characteristics. Sediment samples will also be taken from beneath the canal segments to determine the depth of carbonate leaching. Canal profiles will be examined for evidence of artificial linings as well as the presence of manganese oxides or other evidence of salinization or waterlogging. Special attention will be paid to identifying remnants of canal embankments; if these are present, they will be examined for evidence of canal cleaning and maintenance activities. Finally, canal stratigraphy will be assessed and radiocarbon samples, burned and suspended clay archaeomagnetic samples, and ceramics will be collected where possible, to determine dates for canal segments and sequences of fill.

In addition to the reexamination of those canal segments, the profiles of trenches excavated during the testing program will be studied to determine, wherever possible, the location of the aboriginal surface. Using computer modelling, the depth to caliche, thickness of the solum, and paleotopography of former surfaces will be projected from test trench data.

To the extent possible, the nature of the water distribution system and the stratigraphic relationships between the canals and the various components of the site will be assessed. Known canal segments within the impact area will be correlated with other known canals and extant canal embankments will be examined for evidence of headgates or other distribution features.

The collection and analysis of comparative data for use in interpreting the Las Colinas canal segments will include a variety of topics. Published canal profiles will be compared to identify differences in canal geometry, form, and size, and data pertaining to the grade of canals and local variations will be compiled and evaluated. These data will then be correlated with available information on the geology, soils, and vegetation of the area to identify patterned variation in the distribution, grade, or form of the canals. Canal segments of different ages will be compared to identify possible changes through time in irrigation methods.

Geologic and pedologic information will also be used to evaluate prehistoric salinization, waterlogging, and agricultural potential. Indirect evidence of salinization and waterlogging may be seen in features that may have been constructed to mitigate their effects on soils and agricultural potential.

During the field study, all accessible canal segments in the area will be examined and measured.

Finally, canal studies will be coordinated with concurrent investigations at La Ciudad to gather comparable data on the canals which served the sites.

Thermal-Infrared Sensing

Stratigraphic units present in canals, and in the Las Colinas area generally, are often difficult to discern because of subtle changes in color, texture, and consistency. Traditionally, several means of enhancing the visibility of subtle stratigraphic differences in profile exposures have been used, including drying, wetting, and brushing the profiles, and cleaning them with forced air. Unfortunately, these methods do not always allow differentiation, particularly of unstructured, artificially deposited sediments.

The recognition of complex stratigraphy at Las Colinas may be enhanced by using a portable thermal-infrared sensor (TIR), which is capable of detecting minute variations in thermal radiation, to "photograph"stratigraphic sections and profiles.

Previous experimentation with this method was conducted at the Parris Mound Site in eastern Oklahoma, under the direction of G. R. Muto. That site included an artificially constructed, Caddoan mound, similar in some respects to Hohokam mounds. Minor stratigraphic units, often very difficult to detect, but just as often critical to interpretation of sequences of deposition, were first delineated using traditional methods. The profiles were then photographed with the TIR sensor and the results of the two methods compared. It was found that in most, but not all, instances, the TIR image delineated stratigraphy as well as, or better than, the human eye.

It appears that minor changes in moisture, surface texture, and, to some extent, composition, governed thermal reflectance. The preliminary success of this experiment suggests the efficacy of the method, and its use is therefore proposed on a limited experimental basis for the Las Colinas site.

AZ T:12:38 (ASM)

The excavation methods detailed above for Las Colinas are generally appropriate to AZ T:12:38 as well. Backhoe trenching, followed by machine stripping of part of the plow zone in areas where features are encountered, and then hand stripping of the remaining plow zone and hand excavation of the features will constitute the basic strategy employed at the site. The area immediately to the east of the tested area and the southern margin of the right-of-way corridor will be initial areas targeted for work, in line with the information presented above. In addition, it will be necessary to obtain copies of all the testing program data so that the exact boundaries of the tested area may be established, and so that the testing data may be integrated with the information to be collected at the site.

The specific means for collecting and analyzing the data from AZ T:12:38 (ASM) will be the same as those outlined for parallel research questions to be addressed at Las Colinas and will not be repeated here. This strategy insures that the data gathered will be sufficient to approach those issues and will facilitate comparison of the two sites once the materials are analyzed.

REFERENCES

Abbott, David R.

1982 Technological Stability and Change in Hohokam Red Wares of the Salt-Gila Aqueduct Area. Paper presented at the 47th Annual Meeting of the Society for American Archaeology, Minneapolis. MS, Arizona State Museum Library, University of Arizona, Tucson.

Bandelier, Adolf F.

1892 Final report of investigations among the Indians of the southwestern United States. *Papers of the Archaeological Institute of America*. American Series, 4(2). Cambridge: John Wilson and Sons.

Bohrer, Vorsila L.

1971 Paleoecology of Snaketown. *The Kiva* 36(3): 11-19.

Brooks, Danny

1975 An archaeological investigation of the Queen Creek Floodway Project. *Arizona State Museum Archaeological Series* 66. Tucson: University of Arizona.

Crown, Patricia L.

1981a Analysis of Las Colinas ceramics. In "The 1968 excavations at Mound 8, Las Colinas Ruins Group, Phoenix, Arizona," edited by Laurens C. Hammack and Alan P. Sullivan. *Arizona State Museum Archaeological Series* 154: 87-179. Tucson: University of Arizona.

1981b Prehistoric Water Control and Conservation in South-Central Arizona. Paper presented at the 80th Annual Meeting of the American Anthropological Association, Los Angeles. MS, Arizona State Museum Library, University of Arizona, Tucson.

Douglas, Andrew E.

1938 Southwestern dated ruins: V. *Tree-Ring Bulletin* 5(2): 10-13.

Doyel, David E.

1974 Excavations in the Escalante Ruin Group, southern Arizona. *Arizona State Museum Archaeological Series* 37. Tucson: University of Arizona.

1980 Hohokam social organization and the Sedentary to Classic transition. In "Current Issues in Hohokam Prehistory: Proceedings of a Symposium," edited by David E. Doyel and Fred Plog. *Arizona State University Anthropological Research Papers* 23: 23-40. Tempe: Arizona State University.

Doyel, David E., and Emil W. Haury, editors

1976 The 1976 Salado Conference. *The Kiva* 42(1).

Ferg, Alan

1984 The Junkyard Site (AZ U:15:83). In "Hohokam Archaeology Along the Salt-Gila Aqueduct, Central Arizona Project, Vol. VI: Habitation Sites on the Gila River," edited by Lynn S. Teague and Patricia L. Crown. *Arizona State Museum Archaeological Series* 150(6): 377-490. Tucson: University of Arizona.

Fowkes, Jesse W.

1908 Excavations at Casa Grande, Arizona in 1906-1907. *Smithsonian Miscellaneous Collections* 50: 289-329. Washington: Government Printing Office.

1909 Prehistoric ruins of the Gila Valley. *Smithsonian Miscellaneous Collections* 52, *Quarterly Issue* 5(4): 403-436. Washington: Government Printing Office.

1912 Casa Grande, Arizona. *Twenty-eighth Annual Report of the Bureau of American Ethnology*, pp. 25-179. Washington: Government Printing Office.

Fish, Suzanne K.

1984 The modified environment of the Salt-Gila Aqueduct sites: A palynological perspective. In "Hohokam Archaeology Along the Salt-Gila Aqueduct, Central Arizona Project, Vol. VIII: Environment and Subsistence," edited by Lynn S. Teague and Patricia L. Crown. *Arizona State Museum Archaeological Series* 150(7): 39-52. Tucson: University of Arizona.

Fish, Suzanne K., and Charles H. Miksicek

1982 Sampling guidelines for pollen and flotation. In "Hohokam Archaeology along the Salt-Gila Aqueduct, Central Arizona Project, Vol. I: Research Design," edited by Lynn S. Teague and Patricia L. Crown. *Arizona State Museum Archaeological Series* 150(1): 169-173. Tucson: University of Arizona.

Gladwin, Harold S., Emil W. Haury, E. B. Sayles, and Nora Gladwin
1937 Excavations at Snaketown: Material culture. *Medallion Papers* 25. Globe, Arizona: Gila Pueblo.

Grady, Mark A.
1976 Aboriginal Agrarian Adaptation to the Sonoran Desert: A Regional Synthesis and Research Design. MS, doctoral dissertation, Department of Anthropology, University of Arizona, Tucson.

Grebinger, Paul F.
1971 Hohokam Cultural Development in the Middle Santa Cruz River Valley, Arizona. MS, doctoral dissertation, Department of Anthropology, University of Arizona, Tucson.

Gregory, David A.
1982 The Morphology of Platform Mounds and the Structure of Classic Period Hohokam Sites. Paper presented at the 47th Annual Meeting of the Society for American Archaeology, Minneapolis. MS, Arizona State Museum Library, University of Arizona, Tucson.

Gregory, David A.
1984 Excavations at the Siphon Draw Site. Part 1 of "Hohokam Archaeology Along the Salt-Gila Aqueduct, Central Arizona Project, Vol. IV: Prehistoric Occupation of the Queen Creek Delta," edited by Lynn S. Teague and Patricia L. Crown. *Arizona State Museum Archaeological Series* 150(4): 15-218. Tucson: University of Arizona.

Gregory, David A., and Thomas R. McGuire
1982 Research design for the testing of Interstate 10 corridor prehistoric and historic archaological remains between Interstate 17 and 30th Drive, Group II, Las Colinas. *Arizona State Museum Archaeological Series* 157. Tucson: University of Arizona.

Gumerman, George J., and Emil W. Haury
1979 Prehistory: Hohokam. In *Handbook of North American Indians*, by Alphonso Ortiz. Washington: Smithsonian Institution.

Halseth, Odd
1947 *Arizona's 1500 Years of Irrigation History*. Phoenix: Pueblo Grande.

Hammack, Laurens C.
1969 A preliminary report of the excavations at Las Colinas. *The Kiva* 35(1): 11-28.
1981 Las Colinas—The site, its setting, and excavation procedures. In "The 1968 Excavations at Mound 8, Las Colinas Ruins Group, Phoenix, Arizona," edited by Laurens C. Hammack and Alan P. Sullivan. *Arizona State Museum Archaeological Series* 154: 5-13. Tucson: University of Arizona.

Hammack, Laurens C., and Alan P. Sullivan, editors
1981 The 1968 excavations at Mound 8, Las Colinas Ruins Group, Phoenix, Arizona. *Arizona State Museum Archaeological Series* 154. Tucson: University of Arizona.

Haury, Emil W.
1937 Pottery types at Snaketown. In "Excavations at Snaketown: Material Culture," by Harold S. Gladwin, Emil W. Haury, E.B. Sayles and Nora Gladwin. *Medallion Papers* 25: 169-229. Globe, Arizona: Gila Pueblo.
1945 The excavation of Los Muertos and neighboring ruins in the Salt River Valley, southern Arizona. *Papers of the Peabody Museum of American Archaeology and Ethnology* 24(1). Cambridge: Harvard University.
1976 *The Hohokam: Desert Farmers and Craftsmen*. Tucson: University of Arizona Press.

Hayden, Julian D.
1957 Excavations, 1940, at University Indian Ruin. *Southwestern Monuments Association Technical Series* 5. Globe, Arizona: Gila Pueblo.

Herskovitz, Robert M.
1981 AZ U:9:46—a dual component Hohokam site in Tempe, Arizona. *The Kiva* 47(1, 2).

Howard, Jerry Brian
1982 Hohokam Community Organization at La Ciudad de Los Hornos. MS, Department of Anthropology, Arizona State University, Tempe.

Kent, Edward
1910 Patrick T. Hurley versus Charles F. Abbott and others. Decision and decree filed March 1, 1910. Printed by Salt River Valley Water Users' Association, Phoenix.

Masse, W. Bruce
1976 The Hohokam Expressway project: A study of prehistoric irrigation in the Salt River Valley, Arizona. *Arizona State Museum Contribution to Highway Salvage Archaeology in Arizona* 43. Tucson: University of Arizona.
1979 Hohokam Ceramic Art: Reflections on the Efflorescence and Dissolution of a Prehistoric Southwestern Society. MS, Arizona State Museum Library, University of Arizona, Tucson.
1981 Prehistoric irrigation systems in the Salt River Valley, Arizona. *Science* 214(4519): 408-415.

Midvale, Frank
n.d. Unpublished notes, Book V, Department of Anthropology, Arizona State University, Tempe.
1965 Prehistoric irrigation of the Casa Grande Ruins area. *The Kiva* 30(3): 82-86.
1966 The Prehistoric Irrigation of the Salt River Valley, 4th Edition. Map on file, Department of Anthropology, Arizona State University, Tempe.

Moorehead, Warren K.
1906 A narrative of explorations in New Mexico, Arizona, Indiana, etc. *Phillips Academy, Department of Archaeology Bulletin* 3. Andover, Massachussets: The Andover Press.

Neitzel, Jill
1982 The Issue of Stylistic Variability in Hohokam Research. MS, doctoral dissertation proposal, Department of Anthropology, Arizona State University, Tempe.

Nicholas, Linda
1983 An Examination of Three Prehistoric Canal Systems in the Lower Salt River Valley, Arizona. MS, Department of Anthropology, Arizona State University, Tempe.

Nicholas, Linda, and Jill Neitzel
1981 Canal Irrigation and Sociopolitical Organization in the Lower Salt River Valley: A Diachronic Analysis. MS, Department of Anthropology, Arizona State University, Tempe.

Patrick, H. R.
1903 The ancient canal systems and pueblos of the Salt River Valley. *Phoenix Free Museum Bulletin* 1.

Peplow, Edward H., Jr.
1970 *The Taming of the Salt: A Collection of Biographies of Pioneers Who Contributed Significantly to Water Development in the Salt River Valley*. Phoenix: Salt River Project.

Péwé, Troy L.
1978 Terraces of the lower Salt River Valley in relation to the late Cenozoic history of the Phoenix Basin, Arizona. In "Guidebook to the Geology of Central Arizona," edited by Donald M. Burt and Troy L. Péwé. *State of Arizona Bureau of Geology and Mineral Technology Special Paper* 2: 1-16.

Pinart, Alphonse
1962 *Journey to Arizona in 1876*. Translated by George H. Whitney. Los Angeles: The Zamorano Club.

Plog, Fred
1980 Explaining culture change in the Hohokam Preclassic. In "Current Issues in Hohokam Prehistory: Proceedings of a Symposium," edited by David E. Doyel and Fred Plog. *Arizona State University Anthropological Papers* 23: 4-22. Tempe: Arizona State University.

Schiffer, Michael B.
1982 Hohokam chronology: An essay on history and method. In *Hohokam and Patayan: Prehistory of Southwestern Arizona* edited by Randall H. McGuire and Michael B. Schiffer, pp. 299-344. New York: Academic Press.

Schreiber, Katharina J., Carol Heathington McCarthy, and Brian Byrd
1981 Report of the testing of the Interstate 10 corridor: Prehistoric and historic archaeological remains between Interstate 17 and 30th Drive (Group II, Las Colinas). *Arizona State Museum Archaeological Series* 156. Tucson: University of Arizona.

Schroeder, Albert H.
1940 A Stratigraphic Survey of Pre-Spanish Trash Mounds of the Salt River Valley, Arizona. MS, master's thesis, Department of Anthropology, University of Arizona, Tucson.
1943 Prehistoric canals in the Salt River Valley, Arizona. *American Antiquity* 8(4): 380-386.
1953 The bearing of architecture on developments in the Hohokam Classic period. *Southwestern Journal of Anthropology* 9(2): 174-194.

Sires, Earl W., Jr.
1982 Hohokam Architectural Variability and Site Structure During the Sedentary-Classic Transition. Paper presented at the 47th Annual Meetings of the Society for American Archaeology, Minneapolis. MS, Arizona State Museum Library, University of Arizona, Tucson.
1984 Archaeological investigations at Las Fosas (AZ U:15:19): A Classic period settlement on the Gila River. Part 5 of "Hohokam Archaeology Along the Salt-Gila Aqueduct, Central Arizona Project, Vol. VI: Habitation Sites on the Gila River," edited by Lynn S. Teague and Patricia L. Crown. *Arizona State Museum Archaeological Series* 150(6): 491-726. Tucson: University of Arizona.

Teague, Lynn S.
1979 The Arizona State Museum Cultural Resource Management Division data recovery manual. *Arizona State Museum Archaelological Series* 158. Tucson: The University of Arizona.
1982 The Preclassic to Classic Period Transition in Hohokam Society. Paper presented at the 47th Annual Meeting of the Society for American Archaeology, Minneapolis. MS, Arizona State Museum Library, University of Arizona, Tucson.

Teague, Lynn S., and Patricia L. Crown
1981 *Salt-Gila Aqueduct, Central Arizona Project Archaeological Data Collection Studies and Supplemental Class 3 Survey: 1980-1981 Annual Report*. Tucson: University of Arizona.
1984 Hohokam archaeology along the Salt-Gila Aqueduct, Central Arizona Project, Vol. VIII: Environment and subsistence. *Arizona State Museum Archaeological Series* 150(7). Tucson: University of Arizona.

Turney, Omar A.
1924 *Land of the Stone Hoe*. Phoenix: Arizona Republican Print Shop.
1929 *Prehistoric Irrigation in Arizona*. Phoenix: Office of Arizona State Historian.

Upham, Steadman, and Glen Rice
1980 Up the canal without a pattern: Modelling Hohokam interaction and exchange. In "Current Issues in Hohokam Prehistory: Proceedings of a Symposium," edited by David E. Doyel and Fred Plog. *Arizona State University Anthropological Research Papers* 23: 78-105. Tempe: Arizona State University.

Wasley, William W.
1960 A Hohokam platform mound at the Gatlin Site, Gila Bend, Arizona. *American Antiquity* 26(2): 242-262.

Weaver, Donald E., Jr.
1972 A cultural-ecological model for the Classic Hohokam period in the lower Salt River Valley, Arizona. *The Kiva* 38(1): 43-52.

Wells, Susan J.
1982 The Arizona State Museum Cultural Resource Management Division archaeological analysis manual. *Arizona State Museum Archaeological Series* 159. Tucson: University of Arizona.

Wilcox, David R.
1979 The Hohokam regional system. In "An Archaeological Test of Sites in the Gila Butte-Santan Region, South-Central Arizona," by Glen Rice, David R. Wilcox, Kevin Rafferty, and James Schoenwetter. *Arizona State University Anthropological Research Papers* 18, *Technical Series* 3: 77-116. Tempe: Arizona State University.

Wilcox, David R., Thomas R. McGuire, and Charles Sternberg
1981 Snaketown revisited: A partial cultural resource survey, analysis of site structure and an ethnohistoric study of the proposed Hohokam-Pima National Monument. *Arizona State Museum Archaeological Series* 155. Tucson: University of Arizona.

Wilcox, David R., and Lynette O. Shenk
1977 The architecture of the Casa Grande and its interpretation. *Arizona State Museum Archaeological Series* 115. Tucson: University of Arizona.

Wilcox, David R., and Charles Sternberg
1981 Additional studies of the architecture of the Casa Grande and its interpretation. *Arizona State Museum Archaeological Series* 146. Tucson: University of Arizona.
1983 Hohokam ballcourts and their interpretation. *Arizona State Museum Archaeological Series* 160. Tucson: University of Arizona.

Woodbury, Richard
1960 The Hohokam canals at Pueblo Grande, Arizona. *American Antiquity* 26(2): 267-270.

Yablon, Ronald K.
1980 Archaeological investigations West Papago-Inner Loop sections of Interstate 10, Group 1, Los Aumentos. Final report for test excavations at Group 1, Los Aumentos. Museum of Northern Arizona, Department of Anthropology, Archaeological Contract Section.